FLYING HIGH

BEST WISHES TO MY
GOOD FRIEND, RICH, A VERY
TALENTED GUY !!

"DUKE"

Richard B. Wackrull Jr.

FLYING HIGH

Memoir of a
Thirty Year Adventure

Richard Gould Woodhull, Jr.

This book was printed in the United States of America.

Rev. date: 10/17/2013

To order additional copies of this book, contact:
Xlibris LLC
1-888-795-4274
www.Xlibris.com
Orders@Xlibris.com
141866

Flying High—Memoir of a Thirty Year Adventure

TABLE OF CONTENTS

Foreword

Seventy-nine years ago, I was brought forth by my parents to delight my two older sisters and my younger brother, who came along a couple of years later. When I was only two weeks old, it was decided by my sisters, Carol and Marta, who were three and five at the time, that the new baby would be called "Dukie," and that is what they call me to this day. Others call me Duke.

Throughout my life since then, I have been the undeserving beneficiary of good fortune, blessings of every kind, and just plain good luck at crucial times and circumstances in which, had I lacked those benefits, I would not be here today.

Aside from the religious faith that has sustained me through life, two other special blessings stand out above all of the rest. They exist in the form of two very special women. The first was my Mother, nee Louise Hennen Marsh, a talented and wise person, who—because of some still unexplained sin committed by our Father—launched herself off into the world alone with her four young children when I was five years old. She never remarried, and to make a long story short, she pulled it off brilliantly. She and her story could easily be the subject of a successful TV mini-series. Her example, and the lessons that she imparted personally and through the faith, reason and tradition of our Episcopal faith, have had a strong influence on my life, and that of my brother and sisters.

The other very special person is my wife, Ann, who has been with me for over fifty-five years of married life. She hovers somewhere between sainthood and deserving the Medal of Honor for having endured the difficult life of an Air Force wife during the Cold War and Vietnam, while simultaneously raising two wonderful, productive people—Chris and Ann, our son and our daughter. More to the point, however, is the fact that she has grown and evolved independently through the years, to be even more attractive and exciting now, than she was so many years ago, when we first met. She is a blessing beyond description, for which I am eternally grateful.

Recently, having passed the 79-year milestone of life, I was seized with the idea that I should attempt to create some sort of written record, as an expression of thanksgiving and delight for having lived such an interesting and exciting life to date. If future readers might be entertained or even gain a useful insight or two from my experiences, so much the better. But having neither the intention nor ability to write a full-blown autobiography, I felt that I should focus on a more limited time frame.

So, I have decided to simply write about some of the interesting and sometimes amusing events that occurred during my 30-year career in the United States Air Force. Since Ann and I were married to each other for nearly all of that time, she is definitely an important part of the story.

Chapter One

HOW IT ALL BEGAN

(JUNE-JULY 1955)

In my second year of Air Force ROTC at Florida State University, I received the "Convair Cadet Award," which bestows special recognition on a sophomore. Although I had not yet actually flown as a pilot or even as a passenger, aviation fascinated me. An Air Force flying career held, to me, the irresistible promise of serving my country while experiencing challenge, travel, excitement and even a little danger. My grades were fine, but staying in school away from home was a heavy financial burden, necessitating multiple jobs to make ends meet. Then I learned about, and applied for, the US Air Force Aviation Cadet (AvCad) Program.

The program offered the opportunity for individuals having at least two years of college, and who could meet the rigorous physical, psychological and aptitude requirements, to enter directly into the USAF Undergraduate Pilot Training Program. At the end of that sixteen-month course, the successful Aviation Cadet would simultaneously receive the gold bars of a second lieutenant and the wings of a rated Pilot in the US Air Force.

My initial application had been disapproved, because some albumin appeared in my initial flight physical urinanalysis. Devastated, I thought that my hopes for an Air Force career had ended before they had even begun. But the flight surgeons were prevailed upon to permit a special test—suggested by our family physician—to show that my albumin secretion was a harmless anomaly (called "orthostatic proteinuria"). I passed the special medical test, so several weeks later, although still a civilian, I had a Government-paid commercial airplane ticket to Moody Air Force Base (AFB), Valdosta, Georgia, to undergo the AvCad entrance qualification testing process.

At Moody AFB, about fifteen other prospective cadets and I were subjected to two full days of examinations and tests. It took very little imagination to select the "correct" answers to the written pilots' aptitude test questions. Example: "Which of the following would you prefer to do . . . . (a) spend an afternoon with a good book, (b) work a jigsaw puzzle, (c) take a nap under a tree, or (d) ride a motorcycle at high speed down a winding country road? Tough choice. Another block of questions challenged the candidate's ability to orient himself in space by first showing a drawing of an airplane in the midst of some maneuver, giving additional maneuver instructions, e.g. "roll the wings 90 degrees to the right and drop the nose 45 degrees," and then being asked to select one of four new pictures which would depict the airplane's new orientation. I found the only challenge here was avoiding falling off my chair as I imagined myself executing the required maneuvers.

The activities that eliminated a few candidates were the psychomotor tests. The simplest of these consisted of holding a metal stylus in contact with a small metal circle on a turntable whose speed was constantly changing. Whenever contact was lost, a loud buzzer announced the candidate's deplorable lack of coordination. After five minutes of chasing the dot on the turntable, the total elapsed time "in contact" allegedly indicated my potential for joining Colonel Chuck Yeager as a rated Air Force pilot.

The centerpiece of psychomotor testing, however, consisted of an apparatus in which the applicant was strapped into a movable metal seat equipped with a control stick and rudder pedals. Six feet in front of the seat was a large grid composed of light bulbs arranged in vertical and horizontal rows. When the test began, one of the light bulbs on the grid was illuminated, indicating the candidate's target. Then, guided by a single red light showing the seat's position, I was expected to "fly" the seat with the stick and rudders, until the seat's indicator light coincided with that of the target. Instantly, a new target would appear elsewhere on the grid, and I was off again seeking the new target, with the process being repeated every time a target was reached.

The task was made much more difficult by springs and cables in the system that required varying amounts of pressure to be applied to the stick and/or rudder pedals, depending on the seat's departure from the central, neutral position. During this test, a candidate's coordination— or total lack thereof—was very quickly revealed. I rather enjoyed it, and was convinced that a coin-operated equivalent could generate some serious money in a penny arcade.

After completing the flight physicals late on the second day, we were all released to return to our homes to await the results, and to learn whether or not we had qualified to enter the AvCad Program.

During my three-day stay at Moody AFB, I was housed in the Transient Airmen's Quarters, an austere, WWII-vintage barrack located about two blocks from the flight line. Late on my last night there, all of the other candidates having departed, I was alone in the barracks. I started hearing the murmur of vehicles and the low whine of jet engines of aircraft moving on the air field. Curious, I dressed quickly and left the building, walking two blocks through the darkness in the direction of the sounds, until I was stopped by a chain link fence. There, several hundred yards before me was the approach end of the runway, with the flashing lights and dim outlines of two twin-jet, F-89 "Scorpion" interceptors taxiing onto the active runway, apparently preparing for takeoff.

Suddenly, the lead aircraft ignited his afterburners and started his takeoff roll. The night air was ripped by the most ungodly, incredible sound that I had ever heard—like a huge, mile-long strip of adhesive tape being ripped lengthwise. It was so loud that you actually felt the energy and vibration moving over your entire body. At the same time, the twin exhausts emitted bluish-white, pointed flames nearly the length of the entire airplane that illuminated the entire scene. Before the first aircraft was half way down the runway, it lifted its nose for takeoff, and you could see the blue afterburner flame impinging on the runway as he lifted off. The second F-89 repeated the process only seconds after the first. As the second airplane became airborne and the roar gradually subsided into a low rumble in the distance, the twin exhaust flames suddenly diminished to two pinpoints of white light, as he "came out" of afterburner, and continued his climb out.

During those few moments, I knew the die was cast, I was hooked . . . I would become a pilot in the United States Air Force, or die in the attempt.

Some weeks later, back home again in Miami, a much awaited letter dated 2 June 1955 came from the Headquarters, Flying Training Air Force, Waco, Texas:

> Dear Mr. Woodhull:
>
> The Commander, Flying Training Air Force, takes pleasure in advising you that you have been selected for appointment as an Aviation Cadet. This is the authority for your enlistment in the United States Air Force for a minimum period of two years in accordance with paragraph 65, Air Force Manual 39-9, and assignment to the 3700th AF Indoctrination Wing, Lackland Air Force Base, Texas, to report between the hours of 8:00 AM and 1:00 PM, 5 July 1955, for appointment as an Aviation Cadet and entrance into Pre-Flight Phase Pilot Training Class 57-B . . .
>
> . . . In qualifying for this appointment, you have met the high standards necessarily required by the United States Air Force. It is hoped that you will be successful in realizing an ambition to take your place in the United States Air Force as a rated pilot.

Chapter Two

AVIATION CADET PRE-FLIGHT

(JULY-SEPTEMBER 1955)

Before spending any serious money on pilot training candidates, the Air Force wanted to be sure that the aspirants were sufficiently intelligent and motivated, were physically fit, and had the proper psychological temperament for life as an Air Force pilot. Therefore, US Air Force Undergraduate Pilot Training began with a very demanding three-month "Pre-Flight" Phase at Lackland Air Force Base (AFB), San Antonio, Texas.

As new arrivals, we new cadets of Class of "57-Bravo," were immediately thrust into a rigid, uncompromising life of rules, regulations and routines. An Honor Code and detailed procedures existed for every aspect of our lives, from overall personal conduct, the wearing of the uniform, making our beds, arranging our footlockers, behavior in the mess hall and even what we could say. Our day to day discipline and supervision were managed by the "upper class," i.e. those cadets who had just completed their first six weeks of Pre-Flight. Those upperclassmen, in turn, were supervised by a seldom-seen handful of actual Air Force commissioned officers, young lieutenants, referred to as "tactical officers."

During the initial orientation on the first day, we learned that in all but the academic section, our speech with the upper class was to be rigorously limited. As a general rule, our only "authorized speech" was limited to "Yes, sir," "No, sir," or "No excuse, sir." The only acceptable and authorized response to a "Why" question posed by an upperclassman was, in fact, "No excuse, sir!" Only if the upperclassmen responded, "I want one," would we then be permitted to provide the requested information. In the coming weeks, often an upperclassman would ask a lower classman a "Why" question ("Mr. Smith, why did you fail to report to the Orderly Room at seven, as directed?"), knowing full well that the lower classman had a reasonable explanation for a perceived failing on his part. After receiving the expected "No excuse, sir!" response, the upperclassman would deliberately fail to say the words, "I want one," leaving the lower classman feeling deeply frustrated. Any other utterances to an upperclassman, if not answering a direct question, would have to be preceded by the phrase: "Sir, request permission to make a statement, sir."

Repeatedly, and in every imaginable way possible, the upper class kept the pressure on with endless inspections and challenges, creating uncomfortable situations that were ostensibly intended to instill in us, an ability to control our emotions and cope effectively with frustration. Very early on, however, I came to view those efforts by the upper class as merely a series of "silly games" that would simply have to be endured. That attitude helped immeasurably to reduce the stress and frustration of present circumstances, and it enabled me to look beyond the present. Come to think of it, that attitude has served me well, all through the years. It's what my wife, in later years, has often referred to, as my "PollyAnna attitude."

During the first six weeks, we would be lowly lower classmen, having no rank or status, other than being basic Aviation Cadets, striving to absorb the heavy academic and physical training load to which we were subjected, and coping with the unrelenting psychological, physical and emotional pressure imposed by the upperclassmen.

The first day, after the obligatory shaved head, getting a battery of immunization shots in both arms, and being issued boots, socks, one-piece fatigue uniforms and underwear, my classmates and I were introduced to our new home for the next three months. Our quarters consisted of a large, multi-windowed room (open bay) with thirty steel cots, fifteen to a side, arrayed along the windows, in an open-ceiling

Korean War vintage barrack. At one end of the open bay was a six-foot-high ventilation fan, while at the other end was a single open doorway, opening into a smaller administrative area called the "Orderly Room," that offered access to the outside of the building.

On the floor, at the threshold of the open doorway leading from the Orderly Room into the open bay, was a two-inch-wide, white painted stripe. Moments after first entering the barracks, we were pointedly and forcefully informed of the purpose of that white line. If an upperclassman or—perish the thought!—an actual commissioned officer ever entered the room, the room would *instantly* and loudly be called to "Attention." At that, everyone in the room would instantly cease whatever he was doing, come to a strict position of attention, maintain strict silence, and remain that way until permitted to "carry on." That rule would remain inviolate from early in the morning, until "lights out" at ten in the evening, seven days a week. Making the room come to attention by entering was a special power and privilege that was jealously guarded and exercised by the upper class. Our times in the barracks during the late afternoon and evening hours were constantly interrupted by the room being called to attention because an upperclassman had entered.

Incidentally, the large ventilation fan at one end of the room is well-remembered for an odd reason. Of course, it was used to pull a cooling stream of air through the barracks during the heat of the day. But it lives on in my memory by the fact that, upperclassman would often demonstrate to newly-arrived cadets how their powerful (and newly-acquired) "command voices" could make the fan "ring" simply by calling the room to attention. That capability never failed to "awe" newly-arrived cadets, whose squeaky attempts to obtain the same result were pathetic.

The academics in Pre-Flight covered such subjects as principles of flight, physiological effects of flight, physics, weather, mathematics, military law and customs, and the like. Since none of those topics was terribly difficult and they all related directly to the life to which we all aspired, they were highly motivating.

The physical training consisted of constant running, calisthenics and "close order drill," i.e. marching. Despite the heat of San Antonio in July, I found the athletic aspects of the physical training to be nothing but pure enjoyment. Close order drill, a traditional and effective method of building unit cohesiveness and instilling instinctive responsiveness to orders, was equally interesting. Once mastered, either as one in the ranks or as the leader, close order drill gives the participant a wonderful sense of order and control.

One of the physical confidence-building exercises to which we were subjected very early on, however, caused more than a few of my classmates real difficulty—the infamous "Project Y." One afternoon, when we would ordinarily have run in formation to the large athletic field near the cadet area for calisthenics, we were loaded on buses instead, and taken to a distant field elsewhere on the base, for what we were told was known as "Project Y." Arriving at a large, sawdust-covered field the size of several tennis courts, we gazed up at a strange, but imposing structure. It was a tower approximately fifty feet tall, composed of a series of five progressively higher wooden platforms, or "floors," that were separated from each other by about eight feet, the entire structure being supported by single telephone poles at each of the four corners.

We immediately noticed a curious thing, however. The telephone poles at the corners were slanted outward, and each of the progressively higher "floors" of the tower was slightly larger then the one below. The largest platform of all, was the one on the very top of the structure. As we stood in the sun beside the buses, puzzling over the strange structure, our instructor—an Air Force non-commissioned officer—explained what would happen next.

"You gentlemen will notice that there is a ladder at the left side of the tower. Each of you will, one at a time, use that ladder to climb to the very top of the tower."

There was an audible "groan" from the assembled group, as we looked at the ladder and saw that because of its angle leaning away from the center of the tower, we would have to cling tightly to the ladder as we climbed, to avoid falling off the ladder and plummeting to the sawdust-covered ground nearly forty feet below.

"When you reach the top of the top platform, you will lie on your belly at the edge, and looking down, grasp the iron pipe handles that have been installed just underneath the edge. Next, you will hold onto the pipe, somersault outward and over the edge, and end up *facing outward*, hanging by the pipe, with your feet a foot or so above the level of the next lower platform. To arrive safely on the next lower platform, you will simply have to swing yourself back and forth, dropping inward, down to the next level at the right time. You will repeat the process until you have returned to ground level."

Another "groan" from the crowd. "Facing outward? . . . Damn, they want to kill us!" When it came my turn to take to the ladder, I made my way to the top without any great difficulty. Having been in the Florida State University Circus, I felt reasonably confident that I would be able to hang from the bar without falling. Nevertheless, looking down over the edge of the top platform from that height was truly frightening. I had a brief conversation with myself regarding my professed desire to be an Air Force pilot, and launched myself into space. After a brief moment of panicky disorientation, I found myself safely hanging on the bar, upright in midair. Vastly relieved, I found the experience to be strangely exhilarating and, after a few moments of trepidation, dropped easily down to the next level. Descending, the levels were progressively easier, and by the time I reached the ground, my system was so full of adrenalin, I was ready to do it all over again, this time without using the ladder!

This exercise produced some very interesting, instructive results. Although everyone eventually went through all of the levels and returned safely to ground level, two who had been considered tough and fearless, virtually our informal leaders, nearly froze on the top and were only able to complete the task properly after being cajoled and jeered at by those who had finished. Other classmates who had previously been relative nonentities, won new respect and status by the alacrity and fearlessness with which they had performed. I learned from the "Project Y" experience not ever to judge others too quickly. All in all, the experience gave Class 57-Bravo a powerful feeling of having accomplished something significant, both as individuals, and as a group.

The academics and physical training were relatively manageable, not appearing to constitute a serious threat to my successfully moving on to the first phase of active flying training, called Primary. But the more problematical and difficult aspect of Pre-Flight, and the one that has lived longest in my memory, had to do with the hazing and harassment meted out by our upper class. Indeed, it often seemed that the objective of the upperclassmen in their interactions with us, was to make us so miserable and frustrated that we would become convinced that we had made a serious mistake, that we were not suited or destined to wear the wings of an Air Force pilot, and should therefore resign from the Program.

Infractions of the rules or simply incurring the displeasure of an upperclassman could doom the cadet to the penalty of doing push-ups, assuming uncomfortable positions, or wasting limited and precious weekend hours marching in the hot sun in full dress uniform around the punishment "tour ramp" located behind the cadet area. The rationale for the hazing and harsh treatment, as already explained, was either to create the qualities of forbearance and stoicism in the prospective pilot candidates or to at least bring those qualities to the fore so that they would be apparent to all. I still consider the fact that I went through the entire program without spending so much as one hour on the punishment tour ramp, as being a minor miracle.

To resign as an Aviation Cadet relegated one to the status known as "Self-Initiated Elimination," or nominally to become an "SIE." An "SIE," as the saying went, was "lower than a snake's belly." When the first "SIE" occurred, I was shocked, but thought that at least the poor guy would be gone, and out of his misery. But no, we soon learned that while any "SIE" had to immediately move out of the cadet area, they had to return each day to perform janitorial and landscaping tasks in the cadet area and suffer the pity, scorn and contempt of their former classmates. Furthermore, after the first week we were permitted to wear the starched khaki uniform with blue shoulder boards, but "SIE"s remained always in the one-piece, green fatigues. After our class was graduated from Pre-Flight, the "SIE"s went on to regular Air Force enlisted jobs, to finish out their two-year enlistments.

With the gradual attrition of classmates through "SIE"ing and because of academic deficiencies, the pressure on those remaining gradually increased. As the blazing hot San Antonio summer days wore on, and we became physically and mentally toughened, the upper class perversely intensified the tempo of relentless and mindless "silly games" and petty annoyances. Several simple examples illustrate the point.

The open bay that we lived in contained an average-sized broom closet for cleaning supplies. Behind the door of the closet was a single deep wash basin, a small shelf and light fixture overhead, a broom, a mop, several dusting cloths and some cleaning solvents. Late one evening, a cross-looking upperclassman came into the room and—after the room was properly called to attention—he announced that he was about to perform a no-notice inspection of the broom closet.

"Who is in charge of maintaining the cleanliness of this broom closet this week? he asked in an off-handed way.

"Sir, I am, sir," replied one of the cadets.

"Oh, I see. And how long does it take you to properly get that broom closet in order, Mr. Urich?

"Sir, it usually takes me no more than five minutes, sir!"

"Well then," said the upperclassman, "If it takes one man five minutes, then five men should be able to put it into perfect order in *one* minute!" He then selected five of the cadets whose cots were nearest the broom closet, ordered them into the broom closet, and closed the door—with some difficulty because of the crowded conditions in the closet. Holding his wristwatch close to his face, he elaborately intoned a one-minute countdown, and then opened the door and ordered the cadets to return to their places. When the ensuing careful "inspection" revealed multiple discrepancies, the members of the five-man cleaning crew received a bitter dressing down, culminating in each being awarded a penalty of one hour on the weekend punishment tour ramp. Then, without another word, he turned on his heel and left the room. If looks could kill . . .

In another typical case one evening, nearly three weeks after which none of us had been permitted out of the cadet area, we were granted two hours "leave" to march to a snack bar on the other side of the base. The granting of that privilege was an unexpected and incredibly-attractive blessing, since it would be the first time that any of us had enjoyed any degree of freedom or anything as exotic as a coke or milkshake since arriving at Lackland. The appointed hour arrived that evening, and nearly all of the class formed-up to march to the snack bar. Five of us elected to forego the milk shakes and freedom, preferring to stay in the barracks to write letters, shine shoes, straighten our foot lockers, and study. Big mistake.

After we had enjoyed about thirty minutes of wonderfully productive peace and quiet, one of the upperclassmen appeared at the line of demarcation, and the room was duly called to attention. After giving us "at ease," speaking in a calm tone, the upperclassman expressed some surprise at finding us still in the barracks and not on our first authorized "leave." He solicitously asked each of us what we were doing. Feeling somewhat pleased with ourselves for having chosen duty over pleasure, we each gave our individual responses. Then, still speaking in a calm way, he addressed all five of us:

"Instead of going with your classmates to drink milk shakes and flirt with the girls, you would rather just hang around the barracks, is that right?" To which we all somewhat proudly responded:

"Sir, yes sir." Suddenly, the upperclassman lost his friendly, solicitous demeanor and shouted:

"WELL THEN, THAT'S EXACTLY WHAT YOU ALL WILL DO FOR THE NEXT HOUR!" With that, one at a time, he dragged each man's footlocker to a position under a ceiling rafter, directed its owner to stand on it and then jump upward and seize the overhead rafter. Soon, all five of us were hanging from the rafters, feeling somewhat ridiculous. Mumbling something about "stupid over-achievers" and "I'll be back," the upperclassman departed.

After a few minutes, the first man fell to the floor. Afraid that the upperclassman would return, he rested briefly, and then regained his position on the rafter. After some breathless discussion between the five of us, however, we all decided that we would each return to the rafter only once, and after that, take our chances. That risky corporate decision of defiance gave us a somewhat shaky spark of self confidence. Each of us endured two uncomfortable "hangings" on the ceiling rafter and then kept a nervous eye out for our tormenter's return. He never did.

Still another fairly typical case in which I was also personally involved, occurred just a few days before the upper class was to graduate from Pre-Flight, and my class would become the upper class. While this incident occurred only days before our elevation to upperclassmen status, its outrageous absurdity clearly illustrates the methodology routinely employed by the upper class during the entire first six weeks.

One of the more respected, sharp upperclassman entered the open bay late one evening, this time with a pleasant, smiling face.

Immediately after the room was called to attention, he quickly and in an unusually moderate tone, called out: "Oh, please . . . . Carry on, all of you." Standing next to me and speaking in an unusually cordial manner, he addressed all of us in the room:

"My classmates and I want you all to know that we have been impressed with the performance of your class . . . . Class 57-Bravo . . . and we leave here in a few days, hoping and believing that you all will continue to make us proud. Mr. Woodhull, you in particular, have done very well, so I have decided to give you an opportunity to demonstrate just how capable and resourceful you are."

To say that I was pleased at his words would be putting it mildly. His friendly, almost casual manner and his reference to his own impending graduation, gave us all a delicious foretaste of becoming upperclassmen in just a few days. I furiously marshaled my thoughts to respond to whatever the "opportunity" would be . . . .

"Mr. Woodhull . . . it is nine o'clock on a Saturday morning. You and a few of your classmates are right here in this room . . . . you suddenly hear a shout outside . . . . you run to the window, look up, and see an F-86 gliding down, with thick smoke trailing behind. The pilot is obviously experiencing a serious emergency. You are shocked to see the F-86 make a gear up, flameout landing on the street there (pointing), slide crazily through the bushes and across the lawn, and it finally crashes into the side of this very building, ending up right here in this room! There is smoke coming from the fuselage, and the pilot is trapped inside the cockpit! Mr. Woodhull, WHAT DO YOU DO?"

With my mind racing to include all of the essential emergency actions that I could think of, I started rattling off the obvious first actions . . . .

"Sir, I would immediately remove the crash ax from the barracks wall and break the F-86 canopy to free the pilot, while directing Mr. Pascoe to use the fire extinguisher to fight the flames, and at the same time, I would send Mr. Brown to the Orderly Room to call to the Fire Department . . . ."

As I spoke, I noticed that the upperclassman's demeanor changed quickly from a look of positive expectation, to a look of disappointment, and finally building into something approximating rage.

"STOP! STOP! STOP! Mr. Woodhull, you really and truly disappoint me! I thought you were sharper than that! You are nothing but a "dull thud," Mr. Woodhull! After all this time . . . you seem to have learned NOTHING!"

I couldn't believe what I was hearing. My look of total bewilderment made it plain to all that I had no idea how I had failed so miserably. Slowly, he put his nose in my face and snarled:

"You want to know what's wrong with your answer? In the scenario that I gave you, A COMMISSIONED OFFICER JUST ENTERED THIS ROOM, AND NO ONE CALLED THE ROOM TO ATTENTION!!"

With that, he stalked out without another word. We didn't know whether to laugh or to cry. Upon reflection, I almost have to believe that the upperclassman was, indeed, just having a little fun, considering how close he was to graduating from Pre-Flight. But the inane, stupidity of his feigned anger was typical of the kind of treatment to which we were subjected, throughout the weeks of our being the lower class.

An important aspect of the lower class discipline from the very first week, was the requirement to memorize and flawlessly recite lengthy instructional passages from various military leaders while being shouted at, being given orders to execute "facing movements," and being placed in stress positions, such as standing on one's head. Strangely, such shenanigans often served to firmly imprint the material in my memory. Here's an example of one of my favorites that I can still recite to this day:

> General George Washington's Order on Profanity: "The General is sorry to be informed that the foolish and wicked practice of profane cursing and swearing, a vice heretofore little known in an American army, is growing into fashion. He hopes that the officers will, by example as well as influence, endeavor to check it, and that both they and the men will reflect that we can have little hope of the blessing of Heaven on our arms, if we insult it by our impiety and folly. Added to this, it is a vice so mean and low, without any temptation, that every man of sense and character detests and despises it."

Another lengthy recitation that I had to memorize and recite was Union General John M. Schofield's essay that starts out with the words:

"The discipline which makes the soldiers of a free country reliable in battle is not to be gained by harsh or tyrannical treatment. On the contrary, such treatment is far more likely to destroy than to make an army . . . ." The words "harsh or tyrannical" were shortened to "H & T" by the cadet corps, and from then on, "H & T" was a term universally used by Aviation Cadets to express unfair or abusive behavior. The entire selection, which I admit I can no longer recite completely, contains some excellent insights worthy of officer candidates to emulate. Here is the complete recitation:

> "The discipline which makes the soldiers of a free country reliable in battle is not to be gained by harsh or tyrannical treatment. On the contrary, such treatment is far more likely to destroy than to make an army. It is possible to impart instruction and give commands in such a manner and such a tone of voice as to inspire in the soldier no feeling, but an intense desire to obey, while the opposite manner and tone of voice cannot fail to excite strong resentment and a desire to disobey. The one mode or the other of dealing with subordinates springs from a corresponding spirit in the breast of the commander. He who feels the respect which is due to others cannot fail to inspire in them respect for himself. While he who feels, and hence manifests, disrespect towards others, especially his subordinates, cannot fail to inspire hatred against himself."

* * *

Nearing the end of that first six weeks of Pre-Flight, a number of lower classmen were selected by members of the graduating upper class and commissioned tactical officers, to assume "cadet rank," and fulfill the duties of the upper class "staff," supervising the activities of the lower class. I was promoted to the rank of Aviation Cadet Colonel, wearing four white stripes on the dark blue shoulder boards that were a part of my uniform. When I informed my Mother in a letter that I had become an Aviation Cadet Colonel, I believe she somehow missed the "Aviation Cadet" part, because in her next letter to me, she expressed astonishment at my rapid rise in the Air Force.

The supervision and training of our underclass, I like to think, was a little more humane but just as tough, as that of our upper class. And yet, in spite of my less than complimentary comments about the hazing conducted by my upper class, I have to admit that when they departed, we felt very well prepared to assume our responsibilities as cadet officers. Several members of my Preflight upper class were truly outstanding individuals, worthy of emulation. As a reflection of the ability of individuals to advance in the Air Force based solely on ability—somewhat "ahead" of US society in general at the time—the upper class cadet Wing Commander was an exceptionally sharp, impressive African-American, whose last name was "Parks," and who displayed unmistakable potential for future Air Force leadership. Tragically, he was seriously injured in a T-33 aircraft accident less than a year later, and reportedly had to leave the service. That was a very sad loss, but his example continues to inspire. Another of Parks' classmates, Gerald L. Prather, later attained the rank of major general and was the commander of the Air Force Communications Command. A serious research effort, I am sure, would yield many other examples.

The time passed quickly for us as upper classmen, and those of us with cadet rank, especially, gained some valuable experience in managing a military organization.

My Mother was not the only one surprised by my rank. After graduating from Pre-Flight in September 1955, I was able to travel home to Miami via commercial air before reporting to my first pilot training base. Having a two-hour layover in Pensacola, Florida airport, I was wearing the uniform that I had been directed to wear until reporting to my next station, complete with the four white stripes on blue epaulets of an Aviation Cadet Colonel. It had not occurred to me that in a Navy town like Pensacola, four white stripes can only mean one thing—the rank of a Navy Captain, equivalent to an Air Force full colonel.

At one point, I noticed a very attractive, well-dressed woman who was only a few years older than I, glancing in my direction. After a few minutes, and much to my pleasure and surprise, she approached me, looked into my eyes, and began to speak. I blushingly returned her gaze, and waited for her to speak, but what I heard was not exactly what I had expected or hoped for. She smiled and inquired: "Excuse me . . . . but what exactly *are* you?"

Chapter Three

PILOT TRAINING

(SEPTEMBER 1955-OCTOBER 1956)

Before leaving Lackland AFB, I received orders to Stallings Airbase, Kinston, North Carolina, for the seven-month initial phase of pilot training, called "Primary." Stallings Airbase was located in the middle of the rich tobacco fields of eastern North Carolina, a few miles northwest of Kinston. While Stallings was technically a civilian airfield, virtually all of its flying activity involved USAF Piper PA-18 and North American T-6G Primary trainers operated by the civilian contract flying school there. The only other flying activity that I recall seeing there, was a once-a-week commercial Piedmont Airlines DC-3 flight arrival and departure. Incidentally, "jumping" that inbound DC-3 for a somewhat distant mock gunnery run during a solo flight in the T-6G was a feat achieved by more than one member of my class.

Back in Preflight, the scuttlebutt about Stallings was that the military training for cadets there was very severe, but shortly after arrival, it became apparent that hazing and "silly games" by the upper classmen, while still present, were subordinated to the serious business of learning to fly. A single serious mistake on any one flight, could result in being scheduled for what was ruefully referred to as an "Elimination Ride" with a flight examiner who was empowered to summarily eliminate the student from the program. And that, in fact, did occur more than once.

The barracks to which I was assigned was of Korean War vintage and provided each cadet with a small private room, with the doorway opening to a central corridor containing a gang latrine and shower room. My barracks was located at the northern end of a line of similar barracks, with a dense stand of trees to the northeast, and a mown open field just to the northwest. Less than 100 yards across that field was the north end of the main airfield runway, that ran roughly northeast-southwest.

On my very first night in that barracks, I experienced another one of those incredibly motivating, awe-inspiring moments—much like that night back at Moody AFB, when I had observed the F-89 night takeoffs. It was early evening, and I was in my room getting settled, wondering why no upper classmen had come around to harass us or at least to monitor our activities. Taking a break, I walked outside into the night, and observed the running lights and bright landing lights of an aircraft to my right, approaching to land in a southwesterly direction. I walked out into the open field, to get a better look, and as the aircraft came nearer and lower on final approach and finally glided over the runway end in the dark, I clearly heard the thrilling sound of air rushing around the landing aircraft—now barely-recognizable as a T-6G—and heard the deep-throated rumble and occasional "popping" backfiring of its throttled-back single engine. After the aircraft had passed on to my left, I heard the subdued "scrunch" of the tires on the runway. Moments later and farther down the runway, the airplane advanced its throttle and made another takeoff into the night.

What I was observing, was members of the upper class performing a night landing stage in their T-6G airplanes, in which they learned how to land and takeoff at night, by making repeated touch and go landings. Looking around, I saw many lights moving across the distant night sky, and over the next hour or so, observed many other landings (and a few sudden "go-arounds," or "wave-offs" as my Navy friends would say). Observing and hearing those landings produced such an adrenalin rush, that sleep that night came only with great difficulty, and very late.

Upon our arrival at Stallings, my classmates and I had been issued multi-pocketed olive drab flying suits, and Kelly green baseball caps. The caps came with a metal insignia of the national seal affixed to the front, and we were told that our own personal radio call sign—when it was assigned—should be painted in small letters on the back of the cap, along with an optional identifying symbol. My personal call sign, "Pogo 52," was subsequently painted on the back of the cap, along with an outline of my home state, Florida. Initially, the bill of the cap was left unmarked for a very important reason.

An informal system existed of progressively documenting each cadet's flying accomplishments by painting specific symbols on the bills of their caps, to show the world just how far in training the individual had progressed. As a result, my classmates and I were awestruck the first morning that we stood in formation outside our barracks and saw members of the upper class for the first time, whose caps were festooned with clear evidence of their impressive flying accomplishments. Two lightning bolts on the left side of the bill represented, respectively, the first solo flight and successful final check ride in the PA-18 Supercub. Two lightning bolts on the right side represented, respectively, the first solo and passing of the 50-hour checkride in the T-6G. Finally, additional symbols in the center of the bill completed the series: A railroad track, sun and moon symbols represented the first day and night T-6G solo cross country flights, and a cloud with a lightning bolt through it, indicated successful completion of the final instrument check ride in the T-6G.

The system was an excellent motivational tool, since each and every symbol represented a very substantial and important step in successfully completing Primary.

We flew two different airplanes in Primary. First, in the Piper PA-18, a slightly "souped-up" version of the venerable Cub. We had "dual" rides with our instructor until ready to solo—about eight hours—and then went on to accumulate a total of twenty hours—but nearly always with an instructor. After successfully passing the final checkride in the PA-18, we then went on to the much larger and heavier North American T-6G. Back in the WWII era, the T-6 was called an "Advanced Trainer," but times had changed. It was a single-engine, low wing monoplane, having a 550 horsepower engine, two cockpits in tandem, two main retractable landing gear under the wings and a tail wheel. The T-6 was notoriously difficult to land without ground looping, but I eventually developed a passionate love for the airplane.

Incidentally, my class was the very last Air Force Undergraduate Pilot Training class to fly the T-6. Our underclass flew the more modern North American T-28A. Several months before I graduated from Primary, when my instructor had completed his transition into the T-28, he took me for a ride and I found it, with its tricycle landing gear, to be ridiculously easy to land.

The purpose of the initial PA-18 phase of Primary was to assess the student's overall flying aptitude while teaching the very basic "stick-and-rudder" skills, takeoffs and landings, with little or no exposure to advanced techniques such as aerobatics, instrument flying or navigation. The Primary student's first flight in the PA-18 with his instructor was designed to identify early on, if he had any "fear of flying" tendencies. The quickest and easiest way for that to be determined was simply to climb to altitude and put the airplane into a spin by slowing the airplane to near-stall speed, and then pulling the stick abruptly all the way back while simultaneously pushing one of the rudder pedals as far as it will go. As a result of those actions, the airplane immediately drops its nose and starts a violent, continuous rotation in the direction the rudder was pushed, while descending rapidly. I found the experience to be exhilarating in the extreme, and pleaded with my instructor to climb back up and do it again, but—having achieved his objective—he refused.

The PA-18 phase progressed quickly. One morning, after one landing with my instructor at the Greenville, NC auxiliary field, he ordered me to taxi the airplane clear of the active runway, because—he said—he wanted to get out. That was his way of telling me that I was ready for my first solo flight. He gave me a few words of advice and then departed the airplane. I taxied to the takeoff position, received authorization for takeoff via a green light from the nearby Mobile Control unit, and took off. After climbing out to 500 feet, I turned right onto the "crosswind leg" and continued climbing. Finally, reaching the traffic pattern altitude, I turned right again onto "downwind leg" and began to think about getting myself safely back on the ground again. As I looked down to my right at the runway where I would have to safely land the airplane in the next few minutes, I suddenly thought of the sense of triumph-mixed-with-trepidation that a young mother-to-be must feel. Here I was, all alone in control of an aircraft in flight, and it would be up to me and no one else to make sure it came out all right. In the event, it did, and in a very few weeks, I was moving on to the far more challenging T-6G.

The first time I was permitted to climb up on the wing of a T-6G and look down into the cockpit, I felt as though I were looking down into the Grand Canyon. At first glance, the instrument panel seemed to have all of the complexity of a 747. The T-6 was so much larger, heavier and more powerful than the PA-18, that on my first few rides, I had the sensation of being in an airliner.

Aviation Cadets always moved around the base marching in formation, singing or chanting anything that came to mind. Frequently, we sang a song to the tune of "My Bonnie Lies Over the Ocean":

> The Tee-ee Six Gee is our airplane, constructed of metal and tin,
> A top speed of over one hundred,
> The plane with a built-in headwind . . .
> Gear up, flaps down, the heck with the instructor,
> We're back on the ground!

A curious fact: The "full stall," three-point method was usually employed to land the T-6. Because you had no forward visibility at all while landing, and because the airplane had a tendency to ground loop immediately after touchdown, landings always were a concern. Safely landing the T-6 from the front seat was challenging enough, but landing it from the rear seat (something some students were permitted to do late in the program, following a back seat instrument training period "under the hood") was significantly more difficult. Years later, when first checking out in the very difficult-to-land U-2 high altitude reconnaissance airplane, I was elated to see that the technique used in landing a U-2 was very similar to landing the T-6 from the back seat. My T-6 experience helped a lot.

Being full of youthful confidence, none of us had the slightest concern about our own mortality, or the dangers of the flying profession. That didn't keep some from responding bravely to the local country girls about their cadet status with the line intended to evoke admiration and perhaps a little sympathy, "Why yes, I fly . . . I face death daily in the sky!" The fact of the matter is, however, that my class experienced no fatal flying accidents during our stay at Stallings. We did, however, lose one instructor, who crashed and was killed while performing some unauthorized low altitude aerobatics in a T-6G at a nearby town. That incident was a useful first exposure to the importance of "air discipline."

My instructor, Mr. Robert H. Edwards, was a stocky old North Carolina bachelor in his 50s, with extensive flying experience going back to the 1920s. He had an engaging, low key—almost grandfatherly—manner about him. He was not a "shouter," like some instructors, but his intense gaze, serious demeanor and pronounced North Carolina drawl caused one to hang on his every word. His moves on the controls were always incredibly smooth and never abrupt, and with an economy of words, his oral instructions were perfectly coordinated with the flight maneuvers being demonstrated. He was, in my view, the perfect flight instructor.

Some of his personal teaching techniques were somewhat unorthodox. Just one example, burned deeply into my memory: Checking out for the first time in night landings in the T-6G was a rather scary experience. The T-6G cockpit instrument lighting was extremely primitive, consisting of dials painted with luminous paint, that were made to "glow" dimly by two small lamps mounted on either side of the cockpit. Anytime you reached your hand in front of the either of the lamps, the "shadow" of your hand caused the cockpit instruments to disappear. This was not a good thing, since during your landing approach, as you made your bumpy descent through the darkness toward the runway on final approach, you struggled to maintain the critically important proper safe airspeed, using the hard-to-see cockpit airspeed indicator.

That evening, as we walked in the dark out to the airplane, Mr. Edwards handed me several cardboard Dixie cup tops and a small roll of masking tape. Offering no explanation, he simply said: "Just put these in your pocket where you can get to them." Later, as we climbed up to pattern altitude after completing two touch-and-go landings, Mr. Edwards gave me an order: "OK, Mr. Woodhull, take one of those Dixie cup covers and tape it over the airspeed indicator!"

In disbelief, I did as I was told. He then demonstrated to me how, if necessary, a safe day or night approach could be made without referring to the airspeed indicator, by using such cues as the pitch attitude of the airplane, sound of the slipstream and vertical velocity indicator. After completing two more night landings on my own without using the airspeed indicator, and thanks to Mr. Edward's no doubt unauthorized technique, I felt a greatly enhanced sense of awareness and confidence.

One of my enduring regrets in life, has been my failure to maintain contact with Mr. Edwards after graduating from Primary, to let him know how very much I admired him and appreciated the excellence of his instruction.

Our days consisted of flying in the morning, and academics in the afternoon. Half of the class would become airborne early, either flying solo or with an instructor, en route to one of the three auxiliary fields in North Carolina used by Stallings: Wilson, Washington or Greenville. The other half of the class piled into blue-painted school buses and made their way to the aux fields over country roads. Then, in the second flying period of the morning, they would fly back to Stallings while their classmates who had flown during the first period, took the buses home.

Primary flight training provided a lifetime of unforgettable memories, sufficient to fill a book. Let me recall a very few. One of the most lasting memories was the first time that I was scheduled to fly solo very early in the morning from Stallings Airbase to Washington, NC, an auxiliary field to the northeast. Walking to the airplane alone in the predawn darkness, I felt like a World War I fighter pilot, preparing for the Dawn Patrol over the trenches and broken European landscape. Becoming airborne alone just before sunup, heading northeast toward Washington and chilled by the cold slipstream, I looked down at the still-dark landscape passing beneath the airplane and noticed that the river patterns were clearly indicated by the low clouds, clinging to their surfaces. The powerful feelings of exhilaration, autonomy, freedom and power that came to me then, are very hard to describe.

Another occasion was not nearly so sublime. I was on a long solo daytime cross country navigation flight. I was maintaining straight and level flight, and following the proper procedure, had reduced the propeller speed to the relatively quiet 1600 RPM setting, to conserve fuel. Everything was proceeding normally, flying in a northerly direction in smooth air, when I began noticing a very gradual and somewhat disquieting change in the tone and pitch of the sound of the engine. This could be a precursor to an engine failure, so could not possibly be ignored.

I checked and rechecked, and rechecked again the power settings, and everything seemed in order, but still the engine alarmingly seemed to be acquiring a more "throaty," almost staccato sound. As I fought to remain calm, but began to seriously consider where the nearest emergency field might be, above and behind the aircraft, I suddenly caught sight of an astonishing sight. A huge, single-engine, propeller-driven US Marine Corp A-1E fighter bomber had caught sight of my US Air Force T-6G trainer, and had slowly eased into position behind me. I had never before seen another aircraft anywhere near me in flight, and I nearly had a cardiac arrest. The Marine pilot must have perceived that he had succeeded in giving me a pretty good scare, because very soon thereafter, he departed in an easterly direction. That was the first, and perhaps one of the most severe scares that I ever had in over 30 years and 6500 hours of active Air Force flying.

Finally, a more pleasant and agreeable memory of Primary has to do with the Link trainer instructors. To learn the basics of instrument flying, we first had to spend hours "flying" small enclosed airplane simulators, that, while anchored securely to the floor of a training room, could turn, tilt left and right, and even raise and lower their noses enough to give the student pilot a sensation of flight. All of the instructors just happened to be attractive women—mostly wives of the flight instructors—whose charm, perfume and soft voices were intoxicating and thoroughly enjoyable for bachelor Aviation Cadets. We flew the simulators alone, of course, but after the simulator flight, the instructors showed us tracings of our flight paths and critiqued our performances. Needless to say, we hung on every word, and had many questions and requests for suggestions to improve.

* * *

Activities outside of flying and academics during Primary were very limited. Military parades on Saturdays, physical training and studying, and participation in the base chapel program on Sundays filled all the other available hours. Looking back now, I am amazed that I was so focused and absorbed in the demands of the cadet program, that I had virtually no dates or social interactions with young ladies in the area, for months on end.

On several occasions, I received wonderful care packages from my mother consisting of fresh apples and different kinds of cheese. My classmates considered those offerings to be a little odd, so I received very few requests to share.

The months rolled by, and I continued through the flying program, growing in confidence and enjoying the experience immensely. I can only recall one incident that interrupted that pattern of success.

The incident involved my preparing for a mid-morning solo flight in the T-6G. After my instructor and a classmate had completed an early morning dual flight, I was scheduled to take the airplane on a solo flight the following period. One of the most important pre-solo requirements was to check the rear cockpit (that would be unoccupied during my solo flight) and ensure that there were no loose objects and the seat belt, radio wires and shoulder straps were securely bound so as not to interfere with the flight controls. The last step, of course, was to close the rear canopy.

After accomplishing all of the required checks, I strapped in the front cockpit, started the engine and taxied out for takeoff. Following the required procedure, during taxiing and takeoff, I had my cockpit canopy open—to allow a quick exit from the airplane in an emergency. Receiving clearance for takeoff, I smoothly added power and started down the runway. Just before liftoff, I had an uneasy feeling that something was wrong . . . something sounded different. And just as the airplane lifted from the runway, that feeling intensified into a strong conviction as I became aware of dirt and debris rising from the floor of the airplane passing my face, and felt my helmet being severely buffeted by the slipstream of air rushing into my cockpit, blurring my vision.

In a moment of deep chagrin and embarrassment, I realized that in my hurry and excitement, I had neglected to close and lock the rear canopy. The open rear cockpit canopy, therefore, was dramatically altering the airflow in both cockpits, creating a dangerous situation for me. Moments later, I was mortified to hear the tower call: "Pogo 52, re-enter the traffic pattern and terminate your flight." The rest of the flight was physically and emotionally uncomfortable, but uneventful. Surprisingly, I only received a mild verbal critique on the incident, perhaps because I coped with the problem well, but more likely because the Chief of Training was chagrined at the tower's failure to notice my open rear canopy until after my takeoff.

Graduation from Primary took place in May 1956, and I was off to the second and final phase of USAF Undergraduate Pilot Training (UPT), called "Basic." In those days, student pilots were sent to either one of two different six-month UPT/Basic courses: Basic Single Engine, flying the Lockheed jet T-33, or Basic Multi-Engine, flying the twin-engine TB-25. Since the majority of students in the Air Force pilot training program in those days were ROTC graduates and already commissioned second lieutenants, Aviation Cadets had a reduced chance of obtaining slots in the jet course. For that reason, I was disappointed to find myself assigned to the TB-25 Basic Multi-Engine course at Reese AFB, Lubbock, Texas. As has so often happened in my life, however, that "disappointment" turned into a blessing in disguise. Besides the obvious unique and valuable advantage of flying a more complicated multi-engine airplane as a cadet, the instrument training was more extensive in the TB-25 than in the T-33. Besides, several years later as an already rated USAF pilot, I was able to undergo the special USAF T-33 Jet Qualification Course at Randolph AFB. So, you could say that I had the best of both worlds.

At Reese, the pace and intensity of both flying and "officership" training increased significantly. Flying periods consisted of two students flying with their instructor, then changing seats half way thru the period. Later, two students could be scheduled to fly without an instructor, in what were referred to as "solo" flights. Transition (landings and takeoffs), instrument and formation flying, and navigation formed the core of the flying training.

One of the special thrills inherent in TB-25 training was the power-off, full flap landing that was included in the course syllabus. The pilot flew toward the runway while still at traffic pattern altitude, continuing until the runway was completely out of sight. Then, the throttles were pulled to 'idle' and full flaps were lowered, and a very steep diving Space Shuttle-like final approach was then accomplished.

Since the TB-25 airplane was a twin engine airplane, considerable attention was given to perfecting single-engine procedures. As a result, I had a critically important principle ingrained in my head that saved my life a number of times in future years in many different airplanes. It was, simply, that no matter how alarming a malfunction or emergency situation might be . . . the first and most important thing a pilot must remember to do is FLY THE AIRPLANE. In other words, do not become so distracted by the problem in the cockpit, that you lose control of the airplane and make the situation far worse. As long as accident reports have been written, violation of that simple principle has been cited innumerable times as the fundamental cause of tragic accidents.

The commander of our unit at Reese was Colonel Travis Hoover, one of the famous Doolittle Raiders, who flew a B-25 bombing mission against Japan from a Navy carrier deck in the early months of WWII. He crash landed in China after the raid and returned to serve throughout the war, finally passing away in 2004. I am ashamed to recall that at Reese the colonel was the object of some irreverent if well-concealed cadet raillery due to his allegedly poorly executed takeoff from the carrier. As the story went, his was the B-25 seen in films from the famous raid, that nearly crashed in the ocean because its flaps had not properly been set for takeoff. As far as I know now, the story is untrue, but it gave some comfort to beleaguered cadets who wanted to believe that even heroes can make a mistake.

At Reese, just as during Preflight, a hierarchical cadet officer structure was maintained to manage the Cadet Corps and to mirror the organization and management of a regular Air Force unit, referred to as a Wing. Management of the Wing was the responsibility of the cadets, who would gain valuable skills and knowledge from the experience. All cadet officers in the Cadet Wing were selected by a small cadre of active duty Air Force officers, who were responsible for monitoring all but the flying aspects of cadet activities.

After several months, our upper class graduated, and I and other members of my class were called for interviews to determine who would constitute the new cadet staff to run the Wing for nearly four months, until graduation. In the end, I was selected as the Cadet Wing Commander, with the rank of Cadet Colonel, the senior cadet officer. While those responsibilities certainly increased the pressures, the inherent opportunities to learn and grow were well worth the trouble. My staff and I were able to maintain the required standards of order and discipline by actively anticipating problems and focusing on successful graduation of every member of Class 57-Bravo.

Since graduation from Basic would not only result in awarding the wings of a USAF Pilot, but also a commission as a second lieutenant, the academic program increasingly included "Officership" subject materials. Those course topics included such subjects as the Uniform Code of Military Justice, wearing of the uniform, ethics, financial responsibility and even the importance of punctuality.

Most of the topics were very stimulating and interesting for the soon-to-be-commissioned-officers. But, I well remember that last topic, because the presenter—a slightly overweight, rather disheveled major—arrived in the classroom late. Instead of shrewdly using his tardiness as a teaching moment and dismissing us early, he made excuses and blundered on with a poorly prepared series of platitudes. He certainly made his point, but not in the way he intended.

* * *

On 13 October 1956, my classmates and I received the gold bars of second lieutenants and wings of United States Air Force pilots. I was designated a Distinguished Graduate, a fact that gave me priority in choosing my initial flying assignment, and later resulted in my receiving a commission in the Regular Air Force.

A curious fact about the occasion of my graduation is the fact that my father, who many years before had separated from my mother and who had played absolutely no role in my life ever since, was in attendance. The day before graduation, I went to see him at the hotel, and it was the first time that I had seen him since I was six or seven years old. When I entered the room and saw him after so long, he could only mutter: "You really don't need me in your life!" I could only agree with him in my thoughts, but because my mother had assiduously refrained from making critical remarks about him through the years, I felt no bitterness.

Two weeks earlier, prior to graduation, I was surprised to receive a letter from my older sister, Carol, who had not written me for many months. She announced her happiness at the news that I would be coming home for a month's leave following graduation. Then, after reading further, I learned the true purpose of her letter when she announced "I have found the girl for you."

Chapter Four

LONG DISTANCE COURTSHIP

(October 1956-November 1957)

After pilot training graduation, I returned to Miami for a 30-day leave—the only full 30-day leave that I ever experienced during my 30-year Air Force career. After spending three weeks sailing, relaxing at the beach and visiting with old high school friends, my Mother asked me if I had yet met the wonderful girl that my older sister had found for me. I sheepishly admitted that I had not, but immediately made amends by learning where she was working, and going to meet her. That was unquestionably the wisest and most momentous decision of my life.

When I met Ann in the small insurance office where she was working, the chemistry—at least on my part—was instantaneous. I was immediately captivated by her trim figure, her soft spoken manner, and her incredible smile. She was in her senior year at the University of Miami and was dating someone named George who owned a new convertible, so I felt I was at a decided disadvantage. But her quiet manner and engaging personality fascinated me, generating an insatiable desire to get to know her. As improbable as it is, during that first meeting I had the awesome sense that "this girl may very well be the one."

Looking back, I think that her charms had somehow paralyzed my brain, because our first actual date was to a masquerade party in which we dressed and attended as a Dutch boy and girl. The outfit that I wore that night—complete with shorts and a yellow wig—is something that fills me with disbelieving horror to this day.

Fortunately, I was scheduled for six weeks of C-54 transition training in West Palm Beach following my leave, so I was able to return to see Ann every weekend. Over that time I was finally able to win her over, and when I left for my first permanent duty station, Charleston AFB, SC, she had accepted my Sigma Chi pin as a sign of our commitment to one another. Thirteen months later, we were married.

My initial assignment after pilot training was to the Military Air Transport Service (MATS) 35th Air Transport Squadron of the 1608th Air Transport Wing, flying the four-engine Douglas C-54 transport. Because of my class standing upon graduation from pilot training, I was able to choose that assignment, believing that it would provide challenging flying opportunities overseas and in varied weather conditions. I was not disappointed.

The C-54 transition training at West Palm Beach was thoroughly enjoyable and exciting, since it related directly to my first flying assignment as a pilot in the Military Air Transport Service. Ironically, the C-54 transition curriculum even included one flight in the amphibian SA-16, making water landings on Florida's Lake Okeechobee. The rather dubious logic of that activity was to give us confidence in our ability to ditch the C-54 in the ocean, should such a need arise in the future (!).

Flying the C-54 was easy, but the most challenging aspect of the transition course was to master the aircraft systems to the extent demanded by the instructors. It wasn't enough to simply recite all of the technical parameters and operational procedures. During the walk around inspection of the aircraft before flight, the student was expected to be able to describe the function and purpose of every panel, drain hole or wire visible on the aircraft exterior.

The MATS operations at Charleston AFB provided airlift support to Europe and South and Central America using the relatively modern Lockheed Super Constellation C-121s of the 76th Air Transport Squadron, and the unpressurized, WWII-vintage Douglas C-54 transports of the 35th ATS, to which I was assigned. The crew of a C-54 consisted of two pilots, one navigator and an enlisted loadmaster or flight attendant.

Because the C-54 was unpressurized, its normal cruising altitude was restricted to 10,000 feet or below. C-54 missions therefore often involved long periods of time flying in the weather, which made overwater navigation especially challenging for the lone navigator. For that reason, all newly assigned C-54 co-pilots at Charleston were required to serve as back-up navigators by passing an eight-week specialized course in the navigational equipment and techniques then in use. That extra exposure to the art of navigation proved to be very beneficial, not just at Charleston, but in future flying assignments, as well.

Life as a newly-minted second lieutenant pilot was very satisfying, despite the fact that I was often mistaken for being a navigator, since they were far more common than pilots. Navigators, I should point out, enjoyed far less prestige than pilots. Just as expected, flying the WWII-vintage C-54 for MATS involved challenging flights throughout Europe and South and Central America, often in very adverse weather conditions. Being a bachelor, and the fact that most of my squadron mates were married with family obligations, I found it easy to acquire additional flying time by continuously volunteering for missions without taking the usual post mission days off provided to married personnel. In fact, after only eight months of flying the line for MATS, I accumulated enough flying time and weather experience to technically qualify as a C-54 first pilot. Elevation to that status, however, had to wait until I had been promoted to First Lieutenant.

Being a relatively rare commodity—a very junior second lieutenant, bachelor and pilot—I found myself being scheduled an inordinate number of times during the week to fill available on base simulator training slots. The fact that the base simulators offered only basic instrument practice and approaches to Charleston AFB, made those sessions of only limited value. I therefore suggested to the sergeant in charge that he program the simulators for instrument approaches at foreign locations. After several weeks, I saw that my suggestion had fallen on deaf ears, so I submitted it in written form to the Base Flying Safety Office. Miracle of miracles!! A couple of weeks later when I went for a simulator session, I was gratified to see that practice instrument approaches were being actively promoted for any location that a pilot requested, foreign or domestic. Through that experience, I learned that even a lowly second lieutenant can have a positive influence on things.

Having become engaged to Ann while she finished her senior year at the University of Miami, my social life in Charleston was essentially limited to squadron duties, training and outdoor athletics during the day, and studying and having meals with my BOQ associates in the evenings. Occasionally, when I returned to Charleston in mid-week from one of my overseas trips, I could go down to Base Operations and have a very good chance of catching a hop down to Florida on a transient airplane that had stopped to refuel. The US Navy pilots assigned to the Pentagon/ Anacostia, in particular, become my own personal airline to Miami during post-trip free time. In fact, the first time that I flew an actual low-ceiling radio range instrument approach at Charleston was on a Sunday afternoon returning from Miami in a Navy C-45, whose pilot— looking distinctly nervous and ill-prepared to make the approach—was more than happy to offer me the opportunity to fly it. Having done it multiple times in the simulator, I executed it without difficulty.

Outside of my very infrequent visits to Miami, Ann's and my courtship was carried on mostly at long distance, via letters and phone calls. Only once, during that 13 months, did she come to Charleston for a visit. On one noteworthy occasion, our engagement was nearly terminated by a late night phone call that I received in the BOQ. Her speech was slurred because of having had a little too much wine to drink at dinner with a female classmate and the classmate's father. It was a very brief conversation. That call was almost too much for naïve, "straight arrow" Duke, and the next morning, I confided in Dick Leal, my BOQ next door neighbor, that I feared that I had become engaged to the wrong girl. He wisely told me that I was overreacting, and the episode was eventually forgotten.

One week before I was due to take leave and proceed to Miami for our wedding, I was stuck in Trinidad in the British West Indies. On the return leg of a long trip to several South American destinations, I had come down with a bad head cold. Such a thing can be very serious for someone flying an unpressurized airplane. When we landed at Piarco Airport in Trinidad, I went to the nearby US Naval base and was seen by a US Navy flight surgeon, who promptly admitted me in their five-bed dispensary. So far, so good. But, the flight surgeon then left on a multi-island inspection trip, leaving me under the care of a flinty-eyed, no-nonsense USN Corpsman, who was not in the least concerned about my wedding plans. After three very anxious days, the flight surgeon returned and I was able to make it home in time for the wedding.

We were finally married in the White Temple Methodist Church on Thanksgiving Day, 28 November 1957, 13 months after I had graduated from pilot training. With financial resources extremely limited, Ann and I carefully planned our honeymoon for Nassau at the Royal Victoria Hotel. When our flight departing flight in Miami was announced, however, I was red faced to see that all of the other passengers were college age males—we were traveling to Nassau with the Stetson soccer team, and Ann was the only female on the plane.

Those were the days before huge gambling casinos and throngs of tourists in Nassau. The quaint English ambiance was everywhere, with an open air civil court in session, presided over by a ponderous Black judge in a white judicial wig, the weather in Nassau was perfect, the famous folk singer, "Blind Blake" entertained us, and we even located a very economical Chinese restaurant near the hotel. It was perfect.

Our first home as a married couple was the upper floor of an old Charleston, South Carolina home, occupied downstairs by the owner, an elderly fourth-generation southern lady who still bore a grudge over the Yankees who had carried out the "War of Northern Aggression." When she learned that Ann was born in Virginia, she was overjoyed to be hosting another daughter of the South. The first time that she had us downstairs for dinner as newlyweds, she confided to us: "I simply cannot *abide* Yankees!" Needless to say, my birthplace instantly became Miami, Florida, where I grew up. I never confessed to her that I was born in Summit, New Jersey.

From the very early days of our marriage, I was required often to be away on trips of 8-10 days' duration, so Ann capably handled all of our personal and financial affairs from the start. Her incredibly dedicated and effective performance as a manager of our family affairs through my many absences during the subsequent years of our Air Force years gives the lie to the common term applied by the Air Force for wives: "Dependent." That term, at least in Ann's case, is a complete and utter misnomer. Not only did she nearly always handle all of our financial affairs, but during many years of our Air Force life together, she had to be the "Mom" and "Dad," as well. There are no words to express the admiration and gratitude that I feel for the dedication and love that Ann has shown in meeting the difficult circumstances of being an Air Force wife for many years.

Several months after settling down to our life in Charleston, with me flying the line for MATS and Ann adjusting to the challenges of being an Air Force wife, our lives were changed by an important, but closely-held announcement. That announcement was that a special flying unit to support worldwide operations of the then-highly classified Lockheed U-2 high altitude reconnaissance airplane, was being formed. I had been selected to join the original cadre of the new unit, that would have its home base at Ramey AFB, Puerto Rico, but which would support classified U-2 operations in a number of other locations. The unit would be equipped with specially-configured rescue versions of the C-54 transport, re-designated SC-54.

Chapter Five

U-2 "OPERATION CROWFLIGHT"

(November 1957-June 1960)

After I had been flying the line for MATS for only 18 months to Western Europe and various bases in the Caribbean area and South America, a new assignment unexpectedly came along. Over the next several years, fortuitous and improbable events transpired that would dramatically influence my career and the remainder of our lives as an Air Force family.

One day in mid-1958, I was taken aside and advised that—along with several of my squadron mates—I had been selected for assignment to a special overseas unit that would support a highly classified intelligence-gathering operation. During that initial briefing, we were told only that the new assignment would involve a permanent change of station (PCS) to Ramey AFB, Puerto Rico. Additional details soon followed.

Because of the haste in forming the new unit, I had to precede Ann to Puerto Rico by several months, which meant that she had to remain in Charleston alone, closing out our affairs. As usual, she handled things beautifully and uncomplainingly.

A word about the rationale for the new unit. Early in the Cold War, there was a critical need for technical intelligence on the yields, characteristics and composition of nuclear weapons of other countries. The answers could only be obtained from collection of particulate and gaseous samples of post-detonation radioactive debris deposited in the upper atmosphere from test explosions. For that purpose, the High Altitude Sampling Program (HASP) was being established, to be executed by the Strategic Air Command's (SAC) 4080th Strategic Reconnaissance Wing, equipped with the then-secret Lockheed high altitude reconnaissance U-2 aircraft.

To determine the atmospheric distribution and physical composition of the radioactive material, frequent U-2 aerial sampling missions—informally called "Operation Crowflight"—were to be flown at very high altitude along lines of longitude, north and south from various operating locations (OL), including Plattsburgh, NY, Ramey AFB, Puerto Rico and Ezeiza International Airport, Buenos Aires, Argentina.

Because those single-pilot Crowflight missions would be conducted at very high altitudes over vast oceanic and jungle areas, our unit, the 2157th Air Rescue Squadron, was being formed as a dedicated rescue unit to support the U-2s at their various operating locations. And as an SC-54 Rescue Crew Commander (RCC), I would be responsible for planning and conducting missions that would accompany the U-2s on major portions of their long flights.

It was exciting to be a part of a unit that was in the first months of its existence, and morale was high as a result. Morale improved, of course, once the families joined us. Our first priority was to get the squadron infrastructure in place so that we could generate the flying sorties required for training and qualifying all of the flight crews in the techniques and procedures peculiar to survival and rescue operations. That training included oceanic assessments, search patterns, aerial deliveries of paramedics, precision drops of rafts and other emergency equipment, etc. The pressure was on, because we did not want to delay the all-important high altitude U-2 aerial sampling operations.

Our unit was assigned eight SC-54 aircraft, newly-refurbished versions of the WWII-vintage C-54 transport, equipped with flare ejection chutes, a large side door for aerial deliveries of paramedical supplies and survival equipment, and scanner "blister" windows for enhanced visibility. The basic crew consisted of two pilots, i.e. a crew commander and co-pilot, a navigator, and two or three paramedics. Because many of the flight durations exceeded ten hours, additional crewmembers were sometimes added. Mission profiles of the U-2 Crowflight sorties consisted of an SC-54 launch either north or southbound several hours in advance of the U-2 launch. The far faster U-2 would then launch and fly the same track as the SC-54, overfly it, and proceed to a predetermined turnaround point before reversing course for home. The much slower and lower altitude SC-54 would, likewise turn around at a pre-determined point so as to minimize its separation from the U-2.

During the mission, the SC-54 navigator continuously kept track of the locations of both aircraft, enabling a timely reaction to any emergency experienced by the U-2. Fortunately, over the next two years of operations, we were never called upon to render actual emergency assistance to any of the U-2 Crowflight missions.

Our operational missions out of Ramey took us either north over miles of ocean, or many hours southbound over trackless Venezuelan jungles, where primitive indigenous people who had probably never seen a modern aircraft, eventually lost their fear of us and would run out to retrieve candy bars dropped to them. I have no doubt that we were responsible for creating some "candy bar cults" deep in the South American jungles, counterparts to the Pacific island "cargo cults" that were created during WWII.

Outside of the intense flying activities, my first significant additional duty was to be designated as the OIC (officer in charge) of the Personal Equipment Section. As such, I was responsible for thousands of dollars' worth of expensive mission equipment such as portable radios, survival kits, large air-deliverable million-candle-power flares, 20-man inflatable rafts, binoculars, etc. Since the unit was just being established, in assuming that duty I was dismayed to be presented with a disorganized pile of large unopened shipping containers in a large dusty and windowless storage room at the back of the squadron hangar, and told to organize it all and prepare for a visit by the commander of Air Rescue Service (ARS), sometime in the coming month.

To accomplish that, I had a very inexperienced team consisting of one staff sergeant and four young airmen. What at first seemed like a thankless, daunting task, culminated in a resounding success. Through hard work and "making lemonade out of lemons," we quickly unpacked everything and developed an accurate inventory and maintenance control system. After we rigorously cleaned the entire area, turned the old packing crates into attractive display platforms and prepared professional identification labels and signs, the result was a showcase of excellence that became the talk of the squadron. When the ARS commander inspected us a few weeks later, our efforts received extravagant praise.

For the families, life at Ramey was quite pleasant. The base itself was of WWII vintage, with excellent large buildings, landscaped grounds and attractive tree-lined roads. Everyone lived in base quarters, which were relatively small, concrete non-air-conditioned individual family units, but with jalousied windows that allowed the constant cooling sea breezes to flow through. Most of the squadron personnel were young families, so social activities consisted mostly of backyard parties and occasional events at the Officers' Club. Because of fairly limited incomes, trips off base were relatively infrequent, limited almost exclusively to the nearby town of Aguadilla, which at least provided a diversion, with its small shops.

The nature of the squadron's mission meant that all crewmembers spent roughly one third of their time away from home on 45-day-long periods of temporary duty (TDY) supporting U-2 operations. The most important operating location away from Ramey was at Ezeiza International Airport, Buenos Aires, Argentina. There, we lived at the rather austere airport hotel, set up an OL joint operations section in an isolated nearby building, and launched U-2 and SC-54 sorties about twice a week. Flights from Ezeiza were either northbound over dense Paraguayan and Brazilian jungle, or southbound over the sometimes-frigid South Atlantic Ocean. The repeated TDYs were a burden, but they made our time at home all the more important and pleasurable.

Weekend off duty time in downtown Buenos Aires was very enjoyable, with wonderful food, movies, polo matches to watch and interesting things to see. The city had a very European ambience and all of the fashions were roughly two years ahead of the United States. Elegant buildings and public statues were everywhere. Although Peron had been deposed back in 1955, the Argentine social fabric was still

47

under some stress. I remember once seeing a fully-uniformed general in the Argentine Army delivering an impassioned speech to a large, vocal crowd in a public park.

And on another weekend, as I was climbing the stairs of a subway station, I suddenly sensed searing tear gas in my eyes and was suddenly faced with a crowd of excited people rushing toward me to escape the riot police above. And early one Saturday morning, we were just departing the airport for downtown in a school bus driven by an Argentine Air Force sergeant, when a huge 16-wheeled fuel truck pulled out right in front of us. We crashed into its side with such force that moments after we abandoned the bus the truck actually started leaking fuel onto the pavement. By some miracle, it did not explode and we lived to tell the tale.

An even more serious incident occurred to me in Buenos Aires that had nothing to do with flying, but which could easily have had a tragic result. Our operations offices were located in a two-story structure 200 yards from the hotel, in a somewhat isolated area of the airport flight line. At night or whenever the building was not occupied, the Argentine Air Force provided security in the form of armed guards. Very late one Saturday afternoon when we all had the day off, I had an urgent requirement to go from the hotel to the ops building to retrieve some important papers from the office.

When I departed the hotel on foot in haste, I unthinkingly neglected to bring along with me the plastic-laminated security badge that we had been issued with the black Crowflight silhouette of a crow. When I entered the door at the end of the building and started up the stairs, I was confronted by a very young enlisted member of the Argentine Air Force. Holding the Argentine version of a Sten Gun in front of him, he was wearing boots, a black Sam Brown belt and a uniform of very coarse, thick blue wool material. In my zeal to get the papers, I simply smiled at him and pointed upstairs, completely forgetting about the security badge that I should have had with me. He clearly recognized me as one of the Americans, and I was sure that he had seen me before.

He moved aside without a word as I mounted the stairs, and as I reached the fourth or fifth step, I was shocked to hear a very loud metallic CLANK sound—the unmistakable sound of the gun's receiver inserting a shell into its chamber. I froze immediately and turned to face him. With his weapon leveled directly at me, he said with a rather shaky voice: "No cuervo, no passa" ("No crow . . . no pass!"). With those four words, he had clearly expressed the sum and substance of his instructions. Needless to say, I understood his message instantly, and was more than happy to retreat, offering a rather shaky "Gracias!" as I departed. Discretion was certainly the better part of valor.

Early in February 1959, I was near completing one of those TDY tours and was scheduled to command a redeployment SC-54 flight from Buenos Aires back to Ramey in four days. Since Ann was due to give birth to our firstborn within a week, I obtained permission to let another pilot take my place on that flight, so that I could get home earlier by hitchhiking on a MATS C-124 that had delivered supplies to our OL and that was leaving immediately for Ramey. Eventually, however, the C-124 that I was on experienced maintenance problems enroute, so I ended up stranded in Trinidad. Ironically, this was also where I had been sick and stranded one week prior to our wedding, back in 1957.

Our son, Christopher, was born on 16 February 1959, and I arrived back home on 20 February 1959, unaware that I had become a father. When I arrived at the house, our next door neighbor ran out say: "Hello, *Dad* . . . . you better get over to the hospital!" Ann had suffered through a difficult, 16-hour delivery, but was unfazed, telling me later that my being there would not have helped.

On another redeployment flight from Buenos Aires back to Ramey, I had an engine failure at night while flying over a solid undercast in the vicinity of Belem, Brazil. Seeking an air traffic control clearance to descend through the clouds to make an emergency landing in Belem, I was only able to obtain a heavily-accented and garbled transmission: " . . . . r-roger . . . . call on downwind leg!" I had no choice but to take the risk of descending through the clouds over the ocean, finding the field visually and completing a night time engine-out landing, all without a proper air traffic control clearance.

The next day, after attending an English language church service, I met Robin McGlohn, an elderly former Pan American Clipper pilot, who had lived in Belem since the late 1930s and had founded a timber firm, *Madeiras Gerais* (General Woods). I had lunch with him in his home and greatly enjoyed his aviation memorabilia, photos of himself with Charles Lindbergh, Wiley Post and others. His live-in Brazilian maid was most attractive. Robin was divorced, but asked me to take letters to his wife who lived in Coral Gables, Florida.

At Ramey, we had very little direct interaction with the U-2 personnel, but at the Buenos Aires OL, it was very different. The co-location the U-2 pilots and staffs with us at the Buenos Aires OL allowed me to become intimately familiar with all aspects of U-2 operations. As a pilot, I was fascinated by the high altitude performance of the U-2, the specialized physiological support equipment that it required, the challenge of coping with its unorthodox flight characteristics and most of all, the irresistible appeal of being alone and totally in charge of an aircraft for extended periods at extreme altitudes. That familiarity created an insatiable desire on my part to someday qualify to become a U-2 pilot. However, having absolutely no jet aircraft experience and with little prospect of ever getting any such experience, I knew that the chances of my achieving that goal were virtually non-existent.

That situation was to change dramatically by a series of fortuitous developments over the next couple of years. The initial and very unlikely step in that process related to a senior Air Force officer, Colonel Howard Shidal, the Buenos Aires OL commander from the 4080th SRW. Our first meeting occurred the day after he had arrived in Buenos Aires, on the small local golf course near the airport, *Club Atletico de Lomas*. He was playing with several of the U-2 pilots, approaching us from the opposite direction on the adjacent fairway. I hit a ball that sliced badly to the right, very nearly hitting the colonel. When I approached him to retrieve my golf ball, we were introduced briefly and I could tell that he was not impressed.

About a week later, it was reported that the colonel was severely annoyed to learn of the publication of pictures and a profile of the then-highly-classified U-2 in a small British aviation handbook from a local Argentine bookstore. He angrily asked to see the person responsible for obtaining the handbook . . . and so we had our second meeting. To his credit and my relief, he graciously accepted the fact that the British publication was legitimate.

The irony was that months later when I subsequently felt compelled to express my passionate interest in flying the U-2, he was the only senior officer available with whom I could discuss the matter. In the event, he listened with interest to what I had to say, but pointed out the obvious fatal flaw—lack of jet experience—in my background. In closing our interview he wished me well, saying that he would certainly like to help me in the future if he were able. Those words proved to be prophetic because of succeeding rapidly-moving events.

After several years in South America, the High Altitude Sampling Program (HASP) moved into a new phase and our squadron (re-designated the 64thARS) re-located to Bergstrom AFB, Austin, Texas. From there, our U-2 support flights continued, but operating over Canada from an operating location at Grand Forks AFB, North Dakota.

For this later phase of Operation Crowflight, the U-2s were no longer co-located with us. Instead, they operated out of Minot AFB in the western part of North Dakota, but the mission support concept was essentially the same. So, for another year, we shuttled back and forth between Bergstrom and Grand Forks, supporting the U-2 flights over desolate, uninhabited regions far in the north of Canada.

Although most of that year's flying was relatively uneventful, there were two incidents that might very well have ended tragically, had it not been for Divine Providence. In the first incident, on a dark wintery day, I had just descended through a very low cloud ceiling at Grand Forks AFB and was performing a difficult low altitude visual "circling approach" to land on a snow covered runway. After successfully completing the low altitude maneuver under low visibility conditions, we touched down as planned within 500 feet of the runway end and I lowered the nose wheel to the runway surface.

Suddenly, not more than 50 yards in front of me, a huge industrial snowplow the size of an 18-wheel "semi" drove out into the center of the runway. With the airplane still moving more than 100 miles per hour on the runway, but well below flying speed, there was absolutely nothing that I could do to save the situation. Miraculously, as we watched transfixed, the snowplow reversed course and departed the runway as quickly as it had entered. Mere seconds after he departed the runway, we flashed by, our left wing missing him by just a few yards. We later learned that the snowplow operator had disregarded his instructions to terminate his operations on the airfield if and when radio contact with the tower was lost. He had erroneously assumed that no airplanes would land under the low visibility conditions that existed.

The second incident was a sudden uncontrollable propeller overspeed that I experienced on an outboard engine while enroute from Grand Forks to Bergstrom with a plane full of passengers, one week before Christmas. Usually, overspeed malfunctions of that kind are controllable by reducing the airspeed and feathering the engine. In our situation, however, the proper procedure was ineffectual. The overspeed condition we were experiencing produced such drag on the airplane that even with Maximum-Except-Takeoff power, we could not maintain altitude. Once again, good fortune prevailed. The weather was clear and the civilian airfield at Watertown, South Dakota was visible below, so I was able to complete an engine-out landing without incident.

Because it was only a week before Christmas and our unanticipated arrival at Watertown was covered on the local radio and newspaper, we were inundated with kind invitations for Christmas dinners and other help from the local citizenry. As it turned out, we all took a bus to Rapid City, where our home unit came to fly us home for Christmas.

A year after returning to the US from Puerto Rico, a whole series of extremely consequential developments took place in rapid succession. First, as a result of my having graduated as a Distinguished Graduate from USAF Undergraduate Pilot Training and being further recommended for a regular commission, I was augmented into the Regular Air Force, with a serial number change from AO3065689 to 54637A. That was a very positive career development.

A week or so later, I received advance notice of my selection to report in the Fall of 1960 to the University of Colorado as a student in the USAF Institute of Technology (AFIT) Program. Because the 64thARS had received further move orders, I was given an interim assignment to the Bergstrom Base Operations as a C-47 and T-33 scheduling officer for "behind-the-line" pilots. Then, still later, I learned that the annual Strategic Air Command (SAC) Bomb Competition would be held at Bergstrom. That fact created an incredibly fortuitous set of circumstances for me, since all of the support flying for which I was the scheduler would be suspended for more than a month.

I was already aware of an exclusive six-week T-33 Jet Qualification Course (JQC) that was offered for non-jet-qualified pilots a few miles south, in San Antonio at Randolph AFB. My temporary enforced relief from flight scheduling because of the SAC Bomb Comp, therefore, created an opportunity that I was desperate to exploit. As a result, I took the audacious and somewhat naïve step of making an appointment with the local SAC Wing Director of Operations—a colonel with whom I had had no previous contact—to ask for help in getting one of the coveted slots in the next JQC class.

Incredibly, the colonel actually was acquainted with Colonel Shidal, who was still assigned to the U-2 Wing, the 4080th SRW. Between the two of them (I never learned all of the details), a class quota in the next JQC class was arranged for me. Within weeks, I had become fully qualified in the single engine T-33 as a JQC graduate, thus overcoming the most important impediment to my dreams of flying the U-2. For the moment, however, my orders to AFIT meant that several years in a dull staff job behind a desk would inevitably follow the university studies that were about to begin. That was a burden that I was willing to bear, because a successful Air Force career absolutely required a college degree.

Chapter Six

RETURN TO UNIVERSITY STUDIES

(FEBRUARY 1961-JANUARY 1962)

Back in July 1955, when I entered the Air Force as an Aviation Cadet, I had already completed over two years of college, that is, one year at the University of Miami and a year and one half at Florida State University. After my Freshman year at the UM, the new school president cancelled all but football scholarships, so FSU being a state school was the only option that we could afford. My academic grades were fine, and two highly successful years in the Air Force ROTC Program had definitely pointed me in that direction. In my sophomore year at FSU, in fact, I had even won the 1953 Convair Cadet Award as the top sophomore AFROTC cadet, receiving a model of an XF-92A as a prize. But despite working in the dining halls and also earning a little as a rigger and performer with the FSU Circus, staying in school had become an arduous financial struggle. For that reason, entering the USAF Undergraduate Pilot Training Program as an Aviation Cadet without a four-year college degree was an available and irresistible option.

Now, having accomplished over four years of challenging operational flying, being married and having started a family, securing a solid family future in the Air Force had taken on new importance. It had become painfully obvious that the majority of my peers were college graduates, having graduated either from ROTC or one of the service academies. That realization made it obvious that advancement in my Air Force career would depend on getting at least a bachelor's degree.

Fortunately, the Air Force Institute of Technology (AFIT) Program existed then, in which officer applicants with adequate academic credentials could, if selected, be sent to a civilian university for a year or more of undergraduate or post graduate studies in disciplines that would be applicable to service needs. The downside was the fact that upon graduation, AFIT graduates would inevitably receive a three-year-minimum directed-duty assignment to a headquarters staff job somewhere, sitting behind a desk. For someone who had entered the Air Force primarily to fly, the prospect of having a ground job with only minimal flying each month to maintain currency was not very appealing.

Focusing on the positive side of things, however, and aware that selection for one of the limited AFIT assignments would be problematical at best, I had applied even before leaving Ramey. The announcement of my selection was a complete surprise, as it came directly to us at home in a letter from Headquarters AFIT. The original notification mentioned the University of Chicago, which caused us to make family preparations and conduct research on that area. When the formal orders came weeks later, however, the University of Colorado (CU) School of Business in Boulder, Colorado was designated as our destination.

Although CU may have a reputation as a party school, that was definitely not the case with any of the AFIT students studying there. Any individual who is being fully subsidized as we AFIT students were, inevitably feels excruciating pressure to excel academically. The incredible opportunity of being relieved of normal Air Force duties in exchange for the life of a college student working toward a coveted baccalaureate degree produced in me a compulsion to succeed that bordered on paranoia. So, in the days before the internet and Google, I spent many hours practically living in the University Library, studying and doing the necessary research for all of my courses.

That perceived requirement to academically excel caused me to get off to a shaky start with my faculty advisor. After looking at my previous academic record, my faculty advisor included Trigonometry I on the list of the first courses that I should take. Of all of the academic disciplines, however, mathematics was my weakest, and with the passage of time, I was sure that my meager knowledge of algebra had all but disappeared. At our initial planning meeting, therefore, I was desperately afraid to admit to what he would probably consider to be proof of my academic weakness and lack of potential. I was quite certain, though, that if I attempted to take that course in trigonometry, the results would conclusively demonstrate that he was right. After spending an uncomfortable, sleepless weekend agonizing over the situation, I finally arrived at a difficult, but necessary decision.

When we met again to confirm my first semester schedule, I asked for permission to register for a no-credit remedial algebra course. It was a course you might call "Algebra for Dummies," but it proved to be exactly the right decision. After that one semester of getting up to speed in algebra, I was able to make excellent grades in two other higher math courses. Similarly, I opted to take a beginning typing course that dramatically added to my set of personal skills. Thus, I gained a valuable life lesson, which was simply to avoid silly pride and always focus on the long term implications when making important decisions.

In the succeeding months of academic activity, the value of the AFIT program was born out as I accomplished course work in a variety of subject areas that were directly applicable to my subsequent Air Force assignments. Courses included basic management principles, planning, statistics, accounting, motivational theory, human relations, personnel administration, production control, executive decision-making, and the like. An added advantage of my assignment was the fact that I had the opportunity to take some of the same courses and study with some fellow Air Force students who were pursuing post graduate courses.

One of my graduate level executive policy courses divided students into five-man teams representing companies competing in a virtual market place. Each week, we submitted a series of decisions such as pricing of our product, dollars spent on raw materials, capital goods investments and modes of transportation. The following week, we received computer-generated Income Statements and Balance Sheets for all of the competing companies, and a report on the total market share won by each virtual company. Being several years older than my civilian team mates, I became the "President" of our virtual company by default. After one month, my team's company had achieved an absolutely dominant position in the virtual market. The problem was that one of my civilian team mates—only a Junior—took our success so seriously that it took all of my powers of persuasion to convince him not quit school and become an overnight millionaire. I certainly did not want his aborted college career on my conscience.

On the family front, things were going well. Our son, Chris, was now a healthy toddler who enjoyed his time at an excellent day care center. We did have one unsettling episode, when he took a huge swig out of a bottle of white liquid Pledge furniture polish left unattended for less than thirty seconds. He immediately started gasping, realizing that it wasn't milk. After a quick trip to the emergency room, we learned that the liquid polish was mostly kerosene and would quickly pass through his body, which it did with no ill effects.

Soon after our arrival at CU and situating ourselves in the Married Student Apartments, Ann was lucky enough to be hired as a secretary for the CU Dean of Faculty, Dr. Oswald Tippo, a noted botanist. She found the job to be enjoyable and I could not help but notice the look of wary interest in the eyes of a few of my professors who learned of her position. Study demands and having a very young son limited our social lives, but occasionally we would take a day trip up into the mountains west of Boulder. The first time we did that was a bright sunny day, and we departed Boulder by car wearing light, summer-weight clothes. An hour later, having gained more than one thousand feet of elevation, we were shocked and a little frightened to find ourselves being buffeted by strong winds and with nearly zero visibility in a snow shower. Later, we were always better prepared during our other outings into the beautiful high country.

Air Force policy at that time required that all rated pilots maintain minimal levels of flying activity each month, regardless of their duty assignments. Since nearby Lowry AFB in Denver had a small fleet of T-33 aircraft in which I was now qualified, the AFIT tour provided me with the unanticipated and deeply appreciated opportunity to build single-engine jet pilot experience during my time at CU. Proficiency flying out of Lowry provided a very welcome, although brief, periodic break from the heavy academic workload each week or so. Although at that point it seemed a forlorn hope, I also knew that building single engine jet time would enhance my chances of perhaps qualifying to fly the U-2 someday.

Tragically, two of my AFIT classmates were killed one night, crashing into the ground east of Denver. At night, the lights of the city become a dazzling sprawl of bright sparkling jewels. Off to the east, however, just beyond the Buckley Air National Guard field where we would practice touch and go landings, the area was completely devoid of any lights or habitation, making it a black, bottomless pit. After the accident, it was determined that my classmates had almost certainly inadvertently flown into the ground while maneuvering and descending east of the city to enter the traffic pattern at Buckley. That accident served to remind us all of the awful consequences of a few moments of inattention while flying a jet aircraft.

It was also at about the same time that two other fatal T-33 accidents had occurred elsewhere in the larger Air Force. In both cases, the pilots had ejected from the aircraft successfully at low altitude but then had failed to separate from the ejection seat before hitting the ground. Both accident reports suggested that quicker reactions by the pilots might have resulted in their survival. Determined to increase my chances of surviving any possible future bailout, and because it looked like it fun, I joined a civilian skydiving club at the local Boulder Airport. We used a Cessna 182 aircraft with its door removed, making "poised exits" outside the aircraft, pushing away after standing with my left foot on the entry step, both hands on the wing strut, and the right foot in the slipstream. After half a dozen or so jumps, having enjoyed myself immensely and gaining the desired confidence level, I gave it up. Ann never complained about my skydiving, but her attitude became clear to me one day when she and our son met me in the field where I had just landed. It was then that Chris looked at me and said: "Here goes Daddy . . . . ooooh (making a descending motion with his hand) . . . . splat!"

After nearly a year at CU, we had settled into a very busy but satisfying routine. I was making top grades in all my classes, moving along rapidly toward a bachelor's degree in business administration, and enjoying the flying on the side. I had found the academic environment to be highly addictive and stimulating, and I was even grudgingly looking forward to the challenges awaiting me in the directed duty office job to come. Ann was doing her usual outstanding job as wife and mother, while continuing to enjoy her secretarial job at the university.

But that relative calm was shattered in August of 1961, with the erection of the Berlin Wall. That event and the crisis that followed dramatically increased worldwide tensions and drastically changed our futures. Within weeks, most of my fellow Air Force students and I had received notifications that at semester's end we would be ordered "back to the cockpit" at operational flying units. For me, that welcome news meant not only that I would return immediately to full time flying duty, but that cancellation of the post-AFIT directed duty ground job kept alive the chances of my eventually flying the U-2 someday.

With these new unanticipated developments, getting a college degree would have to wait. Under the circumstances, however, I was more than happy to deal with that slight disappointment. (As it happened, I was able to return to CU on temporary duty in 1965 under Operation Bootstrap to earn my Bachelor of Science degree, with honors.)

Orders finally came in January 1962, announcing that I was to be immediately assigned to Westover AFB, Massachusetts as a KC-135 jet tanker pilot in the Strategic Air Command (SAC). Since SAC was an elite major air command, with responsibility for execution of the Emergency War Orders (EWO) of the nation, and the KC-135 tankers were relatively new, that assignment was most welcome.

Chapter Seven

JET TANKER PILOT

(JANUARY 1962-JULY 1966)

The new assignment in January 1962 kept me in the cockpit and sent me to the elite, highly-regimented world of crew duty in jet tanker operations in the Strategic Air Command (SAC). The following four and one-half years with the 499TH Air Refueling Wing (and later, the 99ARW), Westover AFB, Massachusetts were years of significant personal and professional development.

Through the years, aerial refueling equipment, procedures and tactics had evolved slowly, and introduction in 1957 of the new, jet-powered KC-135 was a significant leap forward.

A slightly larger derivative of the Boeing 707, the KC-135 was equipped with a large cargo door, a refueling boom and other equipment required for the aerial refueling mission. SAC was a unique major air command that was virtually an "air force" within the Air Force, having its own unique procedures, standards and ethos. "Peace is Our Profession" was the command's official motto, and the command's bombers and tankers formed the airborne nuclear weapons delivery leg of the "Triad" of capabilities that sustained the Mutual Assured Destruction (MAD) national defense policy during the Cold War. The other two legs of the "Triad" were ground-launched ICBMs (intercontinental ballistic missiles) and the Navy Sub-launched ICBMs.

I have always believed that human motivation arises from the intrinsic satisfaction one gets from worthwhile, meaningful activity, rather than from financial gain or prestige. For that reason, being a part of SAC during the Cold War years was very fulfilling, despite the personal sacrifices involved.

But before reporting to our new duty station, I went on temporary duty (TDY) for three months of KC-135 transition training at Walker AFB, Roswell, NM., during which Ann and our young son, Chris, went for a visit with her parents in Florida. That was to be a pattern that would be repeated on many occasions during our Air Force years. In fact, it seems as though we were never able to go on regular family vacations. Rather, we were always moving from place to place.

One of the most satisfying aspects of SAC tanker crew duty at Westover was the fact of having integral, numbered crews, in which the same individuals always trained, flew and performed alert duty together. As a result, seamless inflight crew coordination usually developed that greatly contributed to effective mission accomplishment, even under stressful conditions. As an instructor, I never failed to notice how the individual crewmembers of the very best crews had developed an eerie rapport with one another, each anticipating the needs of the other, resulting in minimal use of the interphone system during missions. I always used to say that "the best crews show all of the characteristics of a good marriage."

An additional inherent positive result of the integral crew assignment policy, was the formation of strong friendships and shared interests of the crew family members. During the many ground alert periods, the families would often come together for picnics, and the wives and kids mutually supported each other when the men were away. Contrary to what one might think, handled properly, those relationships did not in any way diminish or weaken the all-important "distance" that always has to be maintained between a superior and subordinate in a military hierarchical environment.

In retrospect, the two most compelling aspects of flying the KC-135 were first, planning and executing heavyweight takeoffs, and second, achieving a safe rendezvous between tankers and receivers in all conditions, especially at night or in weather. Once those two mission elements were accomplished, the rest was relatively easy. True, the actual aerial refueling involved some danger due to the close proximity of modern airplanes moving through the air at high speeds. But once the two aircraft were in contact, the really difficult work was being done by the receiver pilot. All the tanker needed to do was fly straight and level, and be prepared to execute an emergency separation from the receiver—called a breakaway—if that became necessary.

The KC-135 takeoff performance was a special area of concern and required meticulous planning. Prior to each launch, aircraft weight and configuration, runway size and condition, and weather conditions were all used by the co-pilot with multiple performance charts to determine the critical parameters of the takeoff. Factors such as the Maximum Refusal Speed, Critical Engine Failure Speed, Ground Minimum Control Speed all factored in to determining a critical abort decision speed for every launch. Takeoff runs were quite long, with the takeoff committed well before the airplane achieved flying speed. Even for experienced KC pilots, the extended takeoff rolls always provide a thrilling surge of adrenalin.

When launching on missions to escort fighters overseas, we would often have one of the receiver unit fighter pilots onboard with us as passengers. In those cases, the "macho fighter jock" was always encouraged to sit up front in the jump seat between us during the takeoff. Invariably, a look of sheer terror would come into their eyes as the end of the runway approached while we were still very much on the ground, just before we "rotated" for liftoff!

The second major concern in the refueling mission was avoiding a midair collision by successfully rendezvousing with the receiver, regardless of visibility and weather conditions. Obviously, the crew navigator played a primary role is this, but the pilots also, using the radar scope and UHF-DF bearings and specialized tactical doctrine procedures, played key roles as well. Sometimes, adverse weather conditions required both tankers and receivers to make last minute improvisations, but losses of missions due to failure to rendezvous were extremely rare.

The KC-135A model aircraft then in use had a number of performance and safety deficiencies that were gradually corrected in subsequent years through re-engining and various other modifications. In those early days, the airplane had a water thrust augmentation system required for heavy weight takeoffs. To safely perform a heavyweight takeoff, therefore, the procedure was to accelerate to takeoff speed, become airborne, climb to only 500 feet, and then lower the nose to level off and accelerate as rapidly as possible before the 670 gallon water tank ran out, at which time the thrust diminished significantly. After leveling off, you had to reduce the drag by quickly retracting the landing gear, accelerating to a safe wing flap retraction speed, retracting the flaps and continuing to accelerate to a safe climb out speed before continuing to climb.

As a result, people who lived anywhere near a SAC base with '135s, had to endure incredibly loud, low altitude overflights over houses and shopping centers off the ends of the runways. Tragically, back in June 1958, Westover AFB had been the scene of a catastrophic KC-135A crash on takeoff with multiple members of the press aboard, caused by the then-imperfectly understood performance capabilities of the airplane. Taking off heavy with wing flaps set at 45 degrees had made that accident inevitable.

The early KC-135 also had a "short" tail design (later enlarged and given a hydraulic power system) that gave it marginal engine-out performance under some conditions. This presented crews with a curious situation in which tankers losing an engine while taking off on an icy runway with a heavy EWO fuel load would neither be able to abort the takeoff because of excess speed, nor avoid crashing due to loss of control. For several years, SAC crews lived with the knowledge that engine loss at an inopportune moment on an EWO launch from an icy runway would inevitably result in a crash. That concern generated so much controversy that Hq, SAC was eventually forced to hand down a formal pronouncement that went down in history with tanker crews: "SAC assumes the risk." Needless to say, that announcement was received with derisive laughter.

Multiple additional duties made life interesting at Westover. When auto seat belts started getting attention (cars were not so equipped in those days), I did the research and made several presentations in the squadron promoting their use. As luck would have it, one week after the Ops Officer, LTC Jay O. McCall, heard my lecture and had seat belts installed at the Base Service Station, he and his son experienced a rollover accident in their SUV while wearing the new seatbelts. I also acted as coordinator for the squadron Commander's Call, spoke at Dependents' Orientations, wrote articles for the base newspaper, and gave lectures to the Alert Force on various topics of general interest.

At Westover, tanker crew members spent about one week out of each month as a part of the famous SAC Alert Force, maintaining readiness to launch on very short notice to support a predetermined receiver on its EWO mission. Alert duty involved living for a week at a time in a special building—the Alert Facility—located very near the flight line. During that week of alert duty, the crew stayed constantly together, going to training classes and always remaining near the flight line in their own dedicated vehicle, once or twice each week responding to blaring klaxon alarms by rushing to their aircraft which was "cocked" for launch in a securely guarded area.

In October 1962, when I was still a crew co-pilot, the Cuban Missile Crisis took place and as a part of the US strategic deterrent force arrayed against the USSR, every element of our unit became immediately and profoundly involved. It is certainly no exaggeration to say that it was the most dangerous incident occurring during the decades-long Cold War between the Free World and the Communist World lead by the Union of Soviet Socialist Republics (USSR).

It is important to understand what the basic posture was of the SAC bomber and tanker forces during the Cold War, prior to the crisis. At a large number (20-25) of SAC bases throughout the US, about *one third* of the entire SAC B-52 bomber and KC-135 tanker force, was continuously "on alert" 24-hours of every day. It was known as the SAC Alert Force. Every one of those airplanes and crews "on alert" had a specific, pre-planned mission involving a retaliatory attack against the USSR or Communist satellite country.

Being "on alert" meant that the bombers (armed with nuclear weapons) and tankers, were continuously guarded, and were parked in special parking areas near the runways. The flight crews resided 24-hours-per-day, one-week-at-a-time, in special buildings near the airplanes on the flight line, where they could respond quickly to alerts and run to the airplanes, start the engines, and takeoff in a very few minutes. The reason for haste, was the fear that the USSR missiles fired from Soviet submarines off the US coast might attack and cripple the US strategic bomber and tanker forces in just a few minutes.

Practice alerts were constantly conducted, to ensure that the crews could, indeed, get to airplanes and takeoff in the required amount of time. Sometimes the practice alerts would only involve running to the airplanes and starting the engines, while at other times, the airplanes would actually "taxi" down the runway. Less frequently, some tankers would actually be launched into the air, but bombers with nuclear weapons aboard were NEVER sent into the air.

One can imagine the tremendous time, effort and expense—for many years—of maintaining the huge SAC bomber and tanker Alert Force as described above. The reason was very simple: A firm belief by US leaders in the willingness and ability of the USSR to attack our strategic forces. To deter such an attack, we had to maintain a credible and invulnerable capability to respond to any attack from the USSR.

When the missile launch facilities were discovered (by U-2 aerial photography) under construction in Cuba, the US viewed it as an aggressive activity, virtually an act of war. Intermediate range missiles launched from only 90 miles away from the US, would inevitably and accurately hit American cities and bases in a matter of minutes, amounting to an intolerable danger to the US homeland. When actual missiles were detected onboard ships that were approaching Cuba, the situation became very dangerous . . . . something had to be done.

It was then that the entire SAC force—many hundreds of bombers and tankers—was put on alert. A continuous parade of flying B-52 bombers—this time, armed with nuclear weapons—was kept aloft 24-hours each day. Their various routes took them across the Atlantic ocean and into the approaches of the USSR where they could be seen on Russian radar. Each bomber flew a mission that lasted nearly a full 24 hours, and involved multiple refueling contacts from tankers based both in the US and in Europe. When the bomber crews were not actually flying missions, they were actually living on the airplanes, as they sat on the ground, ready to launch. No longer were they living in the special buildings near the airplanes . . . . now they were living INSIDE the airplanes, listening to the radios, ready to react at a moment's notice.

Both SAC bombers and tankers are equipped with small kitchens and bunk beds for emergency use.

In the tanker force, it was the same . . . . you were either actually flying a refueling mission, passing fuel to one of the many passing B-52s, or you were living on the airplane, ready to launch. During the worst days of the crisis, my unit sent out twenty-two (22) sorties each day. Each sortie lasted about three hours and fifteen minutes, and offloaded 113,000 pounds to a single B-52 in about twenty minutes of contact. Do the arithmetic! The effort to prepare that many airplanes every day and transfer that much fuel, involved a "Herculean" efforts and great expense.

The behavior of everyone and interactions between tanker and bomber crews, both on the ground and during refueling on actual missions, was very, very serious. We all knew that we were accomplishing what we had been trained to do, and we were determined to perform our duty well in order to prevent a war with the Soviet Union.

During that period, the atmosphere was unreal . . . . almost like a very "bad" movie. All of the crewmembers wore firearms both on the ground and in flight, and believing that we were very close to actual hostilities, we were very worried about our families. They, of course, were alone in the housing area, and we did not see them for days at a time. Some of my colleagues sent their families to temporarily live in another state far to the north, away from the base, assuming that if World War III started, our base would be one of the first one to be hit.

Another of the strange occurrences during the Crisis was the broadcasting of Communist propaganda messages on the International Time Clock Station, WWV. That station broadcasts a simple time signal on High Frequency (HF), continuously, giving precise time reports for use in celestial navigation. All crewmembers are accustomed to getting "time hacks" on WWV, but it was a genuine shock to hear a loud voice break into the transmission with threats and accusations about how "President Kennedy was going to cause World War III," etc . . . . in English, with a strange accent.

During the Crisis, everyone was hungry for news, and the television networks provided news of developments almost as quickly as did the official sources. Remember, this was before the days of cell phones, so we had only infrequent contact with the families, who in some cases, knew more about what was happening than we did.

Saturday, 27 October 62, was a particularly critical day, because that was the day that a U-2 flown by Major Rudy Anderson, was shot down. Although we did not know it at the time, later we learned that he must have died instantly because, when returned to us, his pressure suit was perforated with many shrapnel holes. On the same day, also not known to the public at the time, another U-2—flown by Major Chuck Maltsby, later to become a friend of mine, had severe navigational problems that caused him to overfly the eastern Soviet Union. Although thought to be deliberate, we learned later that the inadvertent overflight was caused by a mistake the pilot made in performing "grid navigation," a method necessary in the Arctic regions. The situation was saved by the fact that the pilot, realizing he was lost, called for help on an international distress frequency.

During the crisis, behind the scenes and unknown to the public, diplomatic contacts were underway, and President Kennedy and Soviet Premier Krushchev actually exchanged two formal letters. The crisis was finally resolved by Krushchev's making a commitment to remove the missiles from Cuba. The American public did not learn until much, much later, that President Kennedy made a secret commitment in return, never to invade Cuba. At the time, that commitment would have been extremely unpopular with the American public, and it remains somewhat controversial to this day. Fidel remained in power until just recently, and the Cuban people continue to suffer under a Communist regime.

When the Crisis was resolved at the highest level, we crewmembers learned first by being told that the alert was cancelled and most of us were allowed to return to our homes. Some weeks later, President Kennedy visited our unit and chatted with us about the Cuban Missile Crisis. He thanked us for the unit's performance during the very dangerous Crisis. After the Crisis, the SAC Alert Force returned to its pre-Crisis posture, and continued in that posture for several more years. Now, it no longer exists.

One of the senior officers with whom we came in contact during the Westover years was General Alvin C. Gillam II, the commander of the 57th Air Division. General Gillam had flown P-47 fighters in Italy in

WWII. General Gillam flew with our unit on occasion and frequently visited with aircrews on alert. He had a very appealing relaxed manner about him that resulted in strong rapport with the aircrews. However, on one occasion the word was passed that General Gillam was dissatisfied with the appearance of some of the aircrews, and that an official 57thAD letter was on the way expressing that sentiment. When it finally came down, it represented the quintessential leadership style of General Gillam. Instead of a verbose and tedious expression of reproach, his letter went to the heart of the matter with a shrewd and terse single sentence: "One thing that I have learned in my 30 years around airplanes, is that *thems (sic) that looks sloppy, flies sloppy.*"

As mentioned before, my progression from co-pilot to crew commander to instructor status was fairly rapid. In September 1964 during takeoff on my initial instructor pilot check ride, I experienced a very serious aircraft malfunction. Moments before we reached the critical "go-no go" point during the heavy weight takeoff roll, the "Cargo Door Unlocked" warning light on the main instrument panel started blinking. That indicated a prohibitively dangerous situation, since an open cargo door inflight could cause loss of aircraft control. Having completed many hours in the KC-135 simulator and been subjected to every conceivable simulated malfunction, the first thought that flashed through my mind was: "This cannot be happening . . . I am not in the simulator!"

But, in the next fraction of a second, I realized that it really was happening, so—much to the shock of the flight examiner sitting in the left seat—I quickly, pulled the throttles to idle, raised the wing spoilers and started applying the brakes as heavily as the anti-skid system would allow, while making the radio call advising the tower of the high speed abort. As we very gradually slowed from what had been only a knot or two below the critical abort speed, I kept thinking ". . . this cannot be happening!" Fortunately, we were able to slow to taxi speed by the runway end, and after turning off onto the apron, we all abandoned the aircraft, as is required by the flight manual. The fire trucks arrived immediately and kept small fires on the wheels under control. Sure enough, within twenty minutes, so many foot pounds of heat had been absorbed by the brakes and wheels from the high speed brake application that all of the thermal fuses in the wheels opened up, flattening all of the tires. We learned later that the boom operator—not my regular crew boom operator—had improperly closed and locked the main cargo door so that it might, in fact, have come open after takeoff.

In November 1964, two months after upgrading to instructor pilot (IP) status, I was fortunate enough to obtain a slot and finish as a Distinguished Graduate in the prestigious USAF Instrument Pilot Instructor School (IPIS) at Randolph, flying the twin-engine T-39. Several months later, in January 1965, I had the opportunity to take the SAC KC-135 Central Flight Instructor Course (CFIC) at Castle AFB. That course was famous for allowing its student instructors to depart significantly from normal safe flight parameters as a way of giving them confidence in the airplane and better preparing them to cope with mistakes made by their students in the future.

It was shortly after returning from CFIC that I was presented with the most challenging staff assignment that I had ever had. While continuing to fly as a part time instructor pilot, my full time assignment was to be the 99th Aerial Refueling Wing Scheduling Officer. That key job was responsible for producing all of the crew flying and alert schedules each month for the entire refueling wing. To accomplish that task, I worked alone six days each week, with only one enlisted man to assist in the printing and distribution of the published schedules. The complexity of the flight scheduling task was staggering, since it involved aircraft availability planning from maintenance, the basic flight planning (fuel load, duration, offload, receiver data, etc.) for every sortie flown by the wing, coordination of all mission details with the receiver units, assignment of specific crews, and detailing of training requirements to be accomplished by each crew member. Compared to the flying schedule, developing the monthly schedule for crew week-long alert tours was comparatively simple.

All in all, it could truly be said that no one—not even the Wing Commander or Director of Operations—knew as much about what was going on in the Wing, day to day, than I. For a mere Air Force captain, it was an enviable and uniquely powerful position in which to be. Fortunately, I held the job for nearly a year without committing any major mistakes.

By February 1965, our son, Chris, had entered the first grade and was thriving under the disciplined care of the nuns at Ursuline Academy in Springfield, and Ann had been expecting our second child for nine months. Late on the cold, snowy night of 23 February 1965, I was working late in the office when Ann called to tell me she thought it was time to come home. After sitting at home for about an hour, we decided that the contractions were getting close enough and we had better be on our way to the hospital in Holyoke. We drove slowly for 30 minutes over the ice-covered roads, and were greeted at the hospital door by a nurse who put Ann in a wheel chair and rolled her slowly away from me down a well-lighted corridor. I was shown to a waiting room, where I joined two other rather disheveled expectant fathers who were hovering over a large ashtray filled with cigarette butts. They had obviously been there for some time.

Remembering Ann's difficult, 16-hour delivery of our son six years before, I knew it would be a while, so I picked up a *Look* magazine, browsed the articles and engaged in idle conversation with the other two in the room. After about twenty minutes, I observed a male nurse approaching the room and I anticipated routine assurances that all was proceeding well. Instead, he looked right at me and said, "Mr. Woodhull, congratulations, you have a daughter!" Our daughter, Ann Bruce Woodhull, was born only twenty minutes after our arrival at the hospital. The two other expectant fathers gave me a look that said "This isn't fair!" When I finally saw our new daughter a short while later, I was amazed at her perfect features that made her appear to be at least several weeks old.

It was during our tour at Westover that my wife and I had our first serious discussions about leaving the Air Force. Sometime in 1965, I had learned of a tempting opportunity to work for United Airlines as a Boeing 707 flight instructor in Denver, and several of my squadron mates had left for airline or charter company jobs. But we were enjoying the camaraderie and challenges of service life, and were intrigued by exciting educational, travel and operational opportunities in the future. So, despite the storm clouds then forming in Vietnam, we jointly made the commitment to remain in the Air Force for a full career. Besides, by this time, Ann had really found a place for herself in the world as a capable young mother and self-confident Air Force wife. One incident from Westover comes to mind that perfectly illustrates the point.

One day, when I was on alert, the clerk informed me that Colonel McCall, the Operations Officer, wanted me to report to him right away. Eagerly anticipating an opportunity to perform some special assignment, I was surprised and perplexed by the colonel's somber demeanor when I entered his office. After quietly asking me to close the door, he said: "Duke, what are we going to do about Ann?" After I recovered from the shock of that question, he proceeded to inform me that earlier that day, she had received a ticket for speeding on one of the base perimeter roads. But far worse, after learning that the ticket carried a one-month suspension of base driving privileges, she had called the Base Commander's office to forcefully complain about the unjustified speeding citation and the outrageously severe penalty (!). Such behavior by a dependent in the Air Force at that time was beyond shocking.

The eventual outcomes of that episode, however, were memorable. True, Ann's 30-day driving suspension was sustained. But, in tacit admission that her complaint was justified, within a week the 30 miles per hour speed limit on the perimeter road where she received the ticket, was increased to 40 mph. For her willingness to challenge the system, Ann earned the admiration of many of our friends, some of whom had suffered in silence after receiving tickets in the same area. Ironically, many years later, Ann bumped into that same former base commander (who had become a brigadier general) in the BX at Offutt AFB. They had not spoken for at least ten years, but the moment he saw her, he exclaimed: "Oh, hello there Mrs. Woodhull!!!" I have a sneaking suspicion that the speeding episode helped, rather than hurt my career progression.

Early in 1966, destiny smiled on us with an incredibly-exciting new opportunity when I learned of a limited call within SAC for volunteers to attempt acceptance into the U-2 high altitude reconnaissance program. After having nurtured what seemed to be a forlorn hope of flying that airplane since our days at Ramey, I could hardly believe that the possibility had now entered my life. When I initially expressed my intention to volunteer, I was warned not to abandon the tanker world, where I had become established and respected. After Ann and I discussed the possible new direction this might take us if I were accepted, however, we decided to go for it. Therefore, risking the alienation of some senior mentors and against the advice of many others, I began to investigate ways to respond to the call.

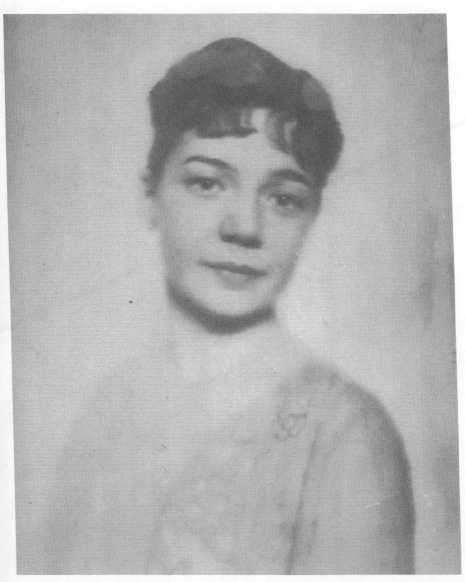

My indomitable Mother, nee Louise Hennen Marsh

My bride on 28 November 1957

FSU Outstanding Sophomore ROTC Cadet 1954

Primary graduate flight cap, Class 57-B

Primary call sign

Crowflight preflight briefing

Family picture 1967

SAC KC-135 Combat Crew T-92

U-2C at Davis-Monthan AFB

MA-1 Partial Pressure Suit

Pulling the pogoes prior to launch

End of a long day

Full pressure suit worn in the R model

Iguaçu Falls 1972

St Patrick's School-1973

Teaching in Rio

Brazilian Air Force AWC Seminar

Rio 1972

Family picture, Fall 1970

Manila

Ann as Sally Cato in *Mame* 1982

Gulo, with her mistress

Singing a duet with Imelda Marcos

Cory Aquino, before the revolution

Special security in the RP Muslim area

Ann honored at my retirement

Chapter Eight

FLYING THE U-2

(July 1966-February 1969)

At the risk of using a horrible pun, I would have to say that the high point in my aviation career was flying the U-2. That is not simply because of the unique characteristics and performance of the airplane. It is, more especially, because of the invaluable operational and staff experience that grew out of the early years flying, and later, managing the employment of the airplane. The self-knowledge gained from the special "003" Cold War survival course undergone as a U-2 pilot was also a uniquely valuable personal experience. I have to add, however, that a decidedly negative aspect of U-2 crew duty was the inordinate amount of time spent away from my family because of the repetitive 60-day tours of duty at our various operating locations.

It would be a mistake to think that my decision to apply for the U-2 was based simply on an immature fascination arising from my previous exposure to the program. As a matter of fact, I had not given it a great deal of thought in recent years, since KC-135 crew duty and associated staff work had been immensely satisfying. But regardless of what airplane he is flying, most pilots sooner or later develop a keen desire to experience the thrill of higher performance, i.e. more speed, greater endurance and higher altitude. And to my mind, the U-2 most certainly offered those things, along with the attraction of a new and different mission, reconnaissance. But, perhaps most intriguing of all, was the special allure of performing classified missions all alone, surviving at extremely high altitudes using specialized physiological support equipment, over vast distances.

In making the final decision to apply, I felt some guilt that I was abandoning the SAC tanker world which had supported me in many ways. I need not have worried, though, because everyone with whom I discussed the matter offered support and encouragement. The only mildly disconcerting counsel was the fear of one senior officer that the move out of the tanker "mainstream" might not be wise from a broad career planning perspective. On other occasions in years to come, as I opted to embark on other assignments that were departures from the norm, I was to receive similar advice. I have never regretted going for the more interesting and challenging options, even though taking that approach no doubt caused me to miss out on achieving flag rank.

The first stage in the application process was for a data package to be submitted to higher headquarters for initial screening of my volunteer statement and service record. It was explained to me that if I passed the initial screening, I would be sent on temporary duty (TDY) to the U-2 unit for personal interviews and other unspecified selection tests. After waiting several weeks, I received orders to travel to Davis-Monthan AFB as a candidate for the U-2 program.

The visit to D-M consisted mainly of informal conversations with the unit pilots and operations officers, as well as some time with the Physiological Support Division enlisted personnel. While I knew I was being closely scrutinized, my overall record, previous support to the unit as a rescue pilot and limited familiarity with the unit from the past gave me a feeling of cautious optimism during the visit.

One of the visit's rather unusual exercises occurred one evening, when I was strapped into the very small U-2 cockpit and left for an extended period in a darkened hangar after squeezing into one of the very tight, restrictive MA-1 capstan partial pressure suits and helmets used in the airplane. Putting that helmet on for the first time gave the distinct impression of forcing your head into an inner tube with a cutout for your face. And when the faceplate was closed and sealed, the wearer was forced to look through the faceplate heating element, a screen-like mesh of wires. The sensation made me think of the unfortunate medieval character whose head was permanently encased in steel.

The darkened hangar exercise was obviously to see if I could tolerate an isolated, claustrophobic environment for some time, and also to give myself a chance to reassess my desire to enter the program. My motivation for the program was also rigorously examined during an interview with one of the unit flight surgeons. None of it, however, dampened my enthusiasm and in just a few weeks, I was informed of my acceptance. We were on our way to Arizona.

Our first impression of Arizona was " . . . wow, look at all this beach . . . where's the ocean?" Before long, though, we came to appreciate the stark beauty and subtle changes in color and texture that occur in the desert throughout the year. The Arizona Sonora Desert Museum in Tucson became one of our favorite places to visit. It was here that our son started school at St. Michael & All Angels Episcopal Day School and Ann had to more frequently assume the role of "Mom and Dad" because of my frequent absences.

I could not help but notice a very somber mood among the squadron personnel on 28 July 1966, the day that I reported in to the U-2 squadron. The reason was soon revealed. Earlier that same morning, one of the squadron pilots, Robert "Deedee" Hickman, had taken off in a U-2C from OL-19 (Barksdale AFB, Shreveport, LA), climbed to altitude, proceeded in a southeasterly direction, and had not been heard from again. Later, we learned that his plane had inexplicably flown all the way to Bolivia before crashing into a mountain there, nearly out of gas. The most probable cause of the accident was subsequently found to be some sort of medical incapacitation. In the next several years that I flew the airplane, we were to lose five more U-2s in accidents through loss of control, but fortunately, none of the accidents were fatal.

The very first thing to do after reporting in to the squadron was to become current once again in the single engine Lockheed T-33. That was accomplished by completing five or six flights and passing a check ride, since all U-2 pilots were required to maintain dual currency in both aircraft. All of our instrument check rides were in the T-33 since no two-seat U-2s existed at the time. Unlike my previous T-33 flying experience, in which both pilots seated in tandem shared the tasks of navigating, making radio calls and controlling the airplane, in the

U-2 squadron the front seat pilot always acted as though totally alone, because that is the way he would be on all operational missions.

As soon I had regained currency in the T-33, the U-2 transition training began in earnest with a week-long ground school to learn the aircraft systems and procedures. Following ground school, the initial qualification ("IQ") flights were scheduled that progressively increased in complexity, finally culminating in upgrade to combat ready status.

With its huge 80' wingspan, removable outrigger "Pogo" wheels under the wings, tandem main landing gear in the belly of the fuselage, wing skids at the wingtips, and a powerful J-75 jet engine in a relatively slim fuselage, the U-2 was a strange cross between an absurdly over-powered glider, and a high performance fighter.

The long, high aspect ratio wings of the U-2 give it the appearance of a jet-powered glider, which might lead one to believe that it is easy to fly. Quite the contrary. The U-2's unorthodox design and performance were strictly optimized for the ultra-high altitude reconnaissance mission, resulting in an aircraft that was difficult and challenging to safely control, both at low and high altitude, and even on the ground. Landing the airplane, in particular, was especially challenging. For that reason, the initial qualification flights were meticulously planned and executed.

The U-2 student pilot in those days had to cope with the fact that no two-place trainer existed. Every flight in the U-2 was solo, and accidents right in the local traffic pattern were not unknown. Because control at low speeds was marginal and landings required a full stall before touchdown, all landings were assisted by a Chevrolet El Camino chase vehicle driven by another U-2 pilot, racing onto the runway behind the landing airplane, radioing height information, e.g. " . . . one foot, . . . six inches . . . hold it off . . . . hold it off . . . good touchdown!"

The first flight by the novice, called IQ-1, could only take place after hours of tutorial conversations with an instructor, and after still more hours of cockpit time becoming intimately familiar with the location of every instrument and switch. My IQ-1 took place on 14 December 1966. Because of the risky nature of that first flight, the winds had to be calm and with no clouds present below 15,000 feet. Pins were installed in the outrigger "pogoes" used during taxiing (sometimes called "training wheels), so they would remain connected to the wings.

To avoid overcontrolling, the takeoff for IQ-1 was accomplished using only partial power, 80% throttle setting. Even at that, the acceleration seemed substantial to the beginner. Before the student took off, his instructor was already airborne in a twin-engine Cessna U-3 "Blue Canoe" that would join up and fly in formation on the U-2's wing, immediately after takeoff. Because of the lack of a U-2 trainer, accompanying the U-2 in the chase plane was the only way the instructor could reliably know the student's airspeed, and assess the quality and steadiness of the student's control.

On the second day that I was in ground school, another pilot ahead of me in the program crashed on his IQ-1 ride. Despite repeated attempts to make a safe approach and landing, he finally lost control and crashed, badly damaging the aircraft. The pilot survived the crash but was washed out of the program. The good news, however, was that some years later, Lockheed was able to build the very first two-seat U-2CT trainer using portions of the wreckage from that accident.

Subsequent IQ flights following IQ-1 gradually had reduced safety restraints, so that the "pogoes" were permitted to fall free of the airplane to the runway during took off, full throttle takeoffs were permitted, and touch and go landings and instrument approaches could be accomplished. IQ-6 was of special significance because that was the first flight in which the student pilot flew fully suited-up in the restrictive MA-1 partial pressure suit and took the airplane above FL600 (60,000 feet).

It was on that flight that the pilot would face the unique high altitude challenge of continuously maintaining precise airspeed control in the very narrow "coffin corner" between Mach buffet and stall buffet for the first time. It was also standard procedure on that mission to deliberately shutdown the engine while above FL600, so that the pilot would experience the full effects of cockpit depressurization and suit inflation. Then, having glided down to a more normal altitude below 40,000 feet, the engine was restarted and a normal descent and landing accomplished.

IQ-7, then, was the first time the fully suited-up novice U-2 pilot would take the airplane to maximum altitude out of the local area and conduct long range celestial navigation and reconnaissance procedures.

My IQ-7 mission took place on the 15th of February, 1967. That mission would be the very first time I would take the airplane above 60,000 feet and leave the local area on a long mission involving celestial navigation and photo reconnaissance. Little did I realize, just how exciting the day would become!

During the previous month, I had accomplished the first five initial qualification flights at low altitude, learning how to takeoff and land the airplane, with its unorthodox ground and flight characteristics.

My sixth U-2 flight had occurred just six days earlier, the first time that I had taken the airplane above 60,000 feet, wearing my skin-tight, claustrophobia-inducing MA-1 partial pressure suit, designed to keep me alive in case of a depressurization. Reaching altitude and looking at the Arizona desert far below, I remember being somewhat disappointed that the terrain below looked about the same as from a jet trainer flying at the mid-30,000 foot range—until I saw a tiny "dot" far below that had a long contrail behind it. It was quite a thrill to realize that I was looking down on a commercial jet airliner, making its way to the West Coast.

Before the descent and landing on that sixth flight, the engine was shut down as planned while still at very high altitude. Then, after restarting the engine at lower altitude, I returned home and landed uneventfully. Just six days later, that training exercise would prove to be invaluable.

The day came for my first long, high flight, "IQ-7." The preliminaries—the special breakfast in the squadron kitchen, the abbreviated flight physical exam, and the rather involved suiting-up process were followed by the ride out to the airplane in an air-conditioned van. The cockpit was so confining and cramped, that I always had the distinct impression of "putting the airplane on," rather than getting into it. But finally, everything was hooked-up, the engine started, and I taxied toward the active runway.

TOWER: *"Spicy 42, cleared into position and hold."* ("42.")
TOWER: *"Spicy 42, cleared for takeoff when ready, winds 090, six knots."* ("Roger, 42.")

. . . Show the ejection seat pins to the accompanying "Mobile" chase vehicle driven by another U-2 pilot . . . Pump and hold the brakes . . . .

Throttle to 80% . . . Check all instruments . . . . Tracker camera "On" . . . .
Release the brakes and push the throttle smoothly to the gate . . . .

On takeoff, the acceleration was so powerful, one had the sensation
of being attached to the end of a gigantic rubber band, and it took a
conscious effort to maintain precise control and avoid the feeling of
being "behind the aircraft." The steep climb-out and departure were
accomplished as planned, the autopilot was engaged, and as the aircraft
passed through 33,000 feet or so, a thick contrail became apparent in
the rear view mirror. Shortly thereafter, as the aircraft passed into the
"Visual Flight Rules on Top, Above 60,000 Feet" area in its climb, I got
busier as the mission's scheduled activities began in earnest.

About two hours later, the airplane was cruising serenely at
maximum altitude, straight and level over the western US in a northerly
direction. It was just minutes after taking a final celestial "shot" of the
sun, to end the day celestial navigation leg. At that moment in time, I
had amassed a grand total of about fifteen hours of flying time in the U-2
and despite the constant attention the airplane required, was finally able
to periodically look around and enjoy the incredible panorama before
me. With a sense of wonder, I gazed far below me at the snowy white,
unbroken deck of clouds that extended as far as the eye could see. Here
I was, in control and mentally well ahead of the airplane, had completed
my first successful celestial navigation leg, and feeling pretty good . . .

BANG!! In a tiny fraction of a second, the airplane experienced
an incredibly violent, high-frequency vibration, accompanied by an
immediate sensation of deceleration. The needle on the cabin altimeter
that constantly displayed the atmospheric altitude inside the cockpit, was
a blur as it spun rapidly upward toward the same altitude as the airplane.
Simultaneously with the flameout, the capstans of my partial pressure
suit automatically inflated, squeezing my body in their life-saving grip,
forcing me into a stiff, hunchback-like posture. Remembering the first
bold print items on the emergency flameout checklist, I simultaneously
pulled the throttle to cutoff and put the battery switch into the
"emergency" position to conserve electrical power.

The first conscious thought that came forcefully to mind in those
first seconds following the flameout, was "Fly the airplane!" For years,
I had always been taught that when confronting any inflight emergency,

the first and most important thing to do is maintain aircraft control. Keeping the wings level, I eased the control yoke forward to avoid a stall, and picked-up the best glide speed. Reaching into the map case to my right, I pulled out a mission planning chart and quickly determined that the nearest suitable emergency field was Kingsley Field, a civilian airfield located at Klamath Falls, Oregon, 122 nautical miles to the west. Notations on the chart provided the important information that the field elevation was 4095 feet above sea level, and the main runway heading was 320 degrees, or roughly northwest.

As I eased the airplane into a left turn to head for Kingsley Field, I rechecked the battery switch in "emergency" to conserve critically-needed electrical energy. That would be needed to keep the helmet faceplate defroster working, to power the minimum essential flight instruments, and to ensure that I would have enough battery power to lower the landing flaps, when they were needed.

SPICEY 42: *"Seattle Center . . . Spicy 42 . . . Spicy 42 . . . MAYDAY . . . MAYDAY . . . I have a flameout . . . am heading for Kingsley Field . . . will not transmit again to conserve electrical . . . request occasional vectors to keep Kingsley at my 12 o'clock, over."*
SEATTLE CENTER: *"Ahh . . . . Roger, Spicy 42 . . . . Seattle Center . . . . Roger . . . Kingsley Field current weather scattered clouds at 1200 feet, 3500 foot overcast, fifteen miles visibility, winds variable, 260 degrees at 10 to 12 in snow showers, altimeter 29.94."*

The situation presented three very distinct possibilities. First, I would continue gliding toward the emergency field until reaching a lower altitude where I would attempt to restart the engine. If successful in getting a relight, I would abort the planned mission and return to home base. That was clearly the most attractive possibility.

Second, despite the clouds, I would hope to eventually catch sight of the airfield early enough to complete an emergency flameout landing. Because of the unknown winds at the various altitudes as I descended and because of my reduced gliding speed, I had to guess that 50 minutes or so would be the elapsed time to the airfield. The marginal weather conditions and fact that I would be landing the U-2 for the first time with no accustomed chase vehicle on the runway to assist with the landing—customary for all U-2 pilots, not just beginners like me—made the second possibility somewhat problematical.

The third and least attractive possibility was simply to eject from the aircraft and take my chances with a winter survival situation until I could be found. Fearing there might be high terrain around the airfield, I decided that the third option would have to be exercised if I hadn't caught sight of the field by the time the altimeter read 5100 feet, or 1000 feet above the Kingsley field elevation. Obviously, an ejection might also become necessary if, while attempting a flameout landing pattern, I realized that I wouldn't reach the runway.

Under ideal conditions, such as excellent visual contact with the runway and light winds, a successful U-2 emergency flameout landing would not be too difficult. Ideally, the pilot would get the runway in sight, drop the landing gear and flaps, and then maneuver to a point called the "high key point," 3000' or more above the intended landing point, flying on the same compass heading as the runway. He would then fly a large 360-degree descending circle to the landing spot. Half way around that turn, after turning 180 degrees, the pilot would reach the "low key" position, at which point he should have lost approximately one half of the altitude, about 1500', and by keeping the runway and intended landing point in sight, could then make required pattern adjustments. Finally, after continuing another 90 degrees after the "low key point," the airplane would arrive at the "270° point," where it should be about 800' above the terrain and close enough to the runway to complete the 360° circle with a final 90° turn to line up with the runway and land.

To guard against possible panicky forgetfulness later, I wrote down and clipped where I could see them, the slightly "rounded-up" numbers "7100" for high key, "5600" for low key, "4850" for the 270° point and "4100" for the Kingsley field elevation. Now, all I had to do, was find the airfield!

As the aircraft descended toward the solid white undercast still far below, the frigid outside temperatures penetrated the cockpit, numbing my hands despite the lined pressure gloves. Gradually, an increasingly dense light frost formed on the cockpit metal surfaces and on the inside of the canopy. Seeking some relief from the cold, and feeling confident that the emergency field was within gliding range, I extended the landing gear to slightly increase the rate of descent. Before long, the tightness of the pressure suit automatically relaxed, making movements easier.

Over a half hour passed, and as I approached an altitude at which a restart might be attempted, I noticed the windmilling engine RPM was lower than I recalled it being during the IQ-6 deliberate engine shutdown a week before. I lowered the nose to increase the airspeed, but the engine RPM did not increase into the permissible range for an engine restart. I made several attempts anyway, but it was no go. We learned later that a large number of engine turbine blades had massively failed, severely damaging the turbine wheel and nearly causing the engine to seize.

Passing through 18,000 feet, I entered the gloom and dim half-light of the overcast, and I felt an unsettling sensation of time acceleration. Like it or not, I was descending into a wintry, hostile environment, and a landing or an inevitable ejection would be occurring in the immediate future. The frosting on the inside of the canopy now seriously impaired my ability to see out, so I began using a plastic, protractor-like device called a "Weems Plotter" as an ice scraper. As I scraped the opaque frost from both sides of the canopy, and searched below to the left and right of the airplane, there was nothing to be seen but solid clouds. It was like descending into a gigantic glass of milk. Finding the field in this mess would be a miracle, and I mentally steeled myself for the unwelcome possibility of having to leave the aircraft.

SEATTLE CENTER (Very weak, breaking up): *"Spicy . . . 2 . . . five miles east of Kingsley . . . . still . . . your 12 o"clock . . ."*

I acknowledged the call and advised that I would be attempting a flameout landing at Kingsley and requested additional position advisories, but received no further transmissions from the Center.

Conditions improved slightly to "between layers" at 12,000 feet, at which time the parachute ripcord "zero lanyard" was re-connected, to ensure a much faster parachute opening in event of a low altitude bailout. Just before that, I removed and stowed the helmet faceplate, always a joyful moment in a U-2 flight. Because the faceplate might not reseal properly, opening it above ten thousand feet was prohibited. After six or seven hours of not being able to scratch your nose or rub your eyes, the pleasure of doing so again was always nearly indescribable.

Now the moment of truth was rapidly approaching. And then a miracle occurred. For a fleeting moment passing through 11,000,' as I was scraping ice from the left side of the canopy and peering downward, I saw a straight line of five blue lights at the dark bottom of a narrow break in the clouds! Those blue lights could only mean one thing: airfield taxiway lights . . . and it was certainly Kingsley Field. This was my lucky day!

Deciding quickly to consider my present position a "high key" point for a landing attempt, I immediately extended the landing flaps and slowed to the proper flameout pattern speed while turning right steeply to 320°, the Kingsley runway heading. As I rolled out, the actual runway became partially-visible, below and to the left. Holding that heading only momentarily, I then started a very gradual left turn, hoping to catch another glimpse of the airfield as I descended to what would be my "low key" position.

Just before reaching the "low key" point after 180° of turn on instruments, I intermittently had brief glimpses of the airfield complex off to the left. But, beyond the "low key" point, I was totally on instruments again. Just before reaching the "270° point," however, the aircraft broke out into the clear. Before me was a windblown winter landscape, and I knew that if I didn't see the runway in the next few seconds, I would have to eject. I looked ahead and to the left where I hoped to see the runway and saw only tree lines and farms. Then I looked farther back to the left, and there it was! The approach end of the runway was fairly close, but I had overshot badly to the right.

As carefully and gently as I could, I banked steeply to the left while diving slightly to maintain airspeed to avoid a stall. There was a crosswind from the left as I rolled out, still diving slightly, toward Kingsley Field's Runway 32. I crossed the runway threshold at five or ten feet, but with 20-25 knots excess airspeed. It was moments later that I experienced another piece of incredibly good luck. As I continued down the runway waiting for the excessive airspeed to bleed off as required for a full stall landing, the large main landing gear made almost-imperceptible contact with the runway. That inadvertent "kissing" of the runway gave me that critically-needed height-above-the-runway information that I had, until then, always received from a chase vehicle racing on the runway behind me. What followed was a normal full stall landing, but with a fairly stiff left crosswind.

The powerless airplane rolled to a stop on the centerline of the runway, 5000' feet from the approach end, with its left wingtip skid touching the runway surface. Reported weather at the time of landing was 1200 feet scattered, 2800 feet overcast, five miles visibility in light snow, with winds 250 degrees at eight knots, gusting to 13 knots.

With the adrenalin still flowing, I felt a surge of thankfulness for the dedication of my instructors for their excellent training, and for a benevolent Creator who had blessed me with a year's worth of good luck, all in one day!

With this day's events, I had qualified for the 349th Strategic Reconnaissance Squadron's very exclusive "Silent Birdman" club. More importantly, because of the happy outcome of the episode, the US Air Force was spared the loss of one of its unique and valuable U-2 aircraft.

There are two aspects of the episode that "rankle" to this day. One was that the local press where I landed erroneously reported that I had performed a "precautionary" landing. Obviously, when you are completely flamed-out, it is definitely not precautionary. The second frustration occurred in March 1968, when the US Air Force *FLYING SAFETY Magazine* recognized my flameout landing with their prestigious "WELL DONE" Award. In the headline, however, my first name was misspelled "Willard," instead of the correct "Richard", with letters one inch high!

I might also mention that Francis Gary Powers once sent me a note regarding that event. We had met several times at pilots' meetings after his return from prison in the USSR. Sometime in 1970, he sent me a copy of his newly-published book, *Operation Overflight* and included the following dedication: "Dear Duke, Best of luck to a fellow U-bird pilot—and a damn good one. Still don't know how you got that one in to Kingsley Field. (signed) Francis Gary Powers Aug 11, 1970."

I could get myself in a lot of trouble if I were to provide details about the operational missions that I flew, once I was combat ready. There is no denying, however, that flying high and alone over denied territory for hours at a time was a very satisfying and exciting thing to do. But sometimes the noteworthy moments had nothing to do with potentially unfriendly people below.

My very first flight from OL-20 at Bien Hoa AB, Vietnam is a case in point. Since that flight would be my first in that operational area, it was to be a simple orientation flight at altitude, but without any photography or other operational activity. Bien Hoa AB, a Vietnamese Air Force (VNAF) installation located about 20 miles north of Saigon, was host to many aircraft with wildly different performance characteristics. Besides our U-2Cs that were ludicrously slow in the traffic pattern, aircraft operating there included the VNAF A-1Es, high speed F-100F *Fast FACs*, A-37 ground attack fighters, slower twin—engine C-123 *Ranch Hand* defoliant dispensers, turbo-prop C-130 *Hercules* transports and the occasional Cessna O-2 lightplane. Because of the diverse aircraft types, the constant high volume of traffic, and because of the necessity to make steep approaches due to possible small arms fire from the jungle area across the river from the base, the traffic pattern at Bien Hoa was a nightmare. And that fact became a critical element in the emergency that faced me less than five minutes after I launched that morning.

A minute or so after takeoff and during the steep climb out, I looked back at the field and saw that the OL-20 vehicles that had accompanied me onto the runway to support the launch had all departed the flight line, most likely heading for the mess hall for a late breakfast. At the same time, I was not surprised to observe the usual swarm of diverse airborne aircraft in and around the airfield. A minute or so later, a very unwelcome cockpit indication suddenly appeared. It was the red "Fuel Low Level" light, indicating that the fuel was not feeding from the wings as it should, telling me that I had mere minutes to get the airplane back on the ground before the engine would flameout. I immediately keyed the radio to advise the tower of my emergency, but found the UHF radio had failed. I switched frequency to the OL-20 launch vehicle, but was still unable to make any contact.

As a result, I had no recourse but to prepare for the unanticipated landing, glide down and enter that horrendous traffic pattern with no radios, praying that no one would run into me, and hope that I could safely land the airplane without the usual height-above-the-runway cues from the mobile vehicle speeding down the runway behind me. I completed the landing without incident, but came to a stop with one wingtip unavoidably dragging on the runway because the "pogoes" were no longer on the wings. That closed the runway for several minutes much to the chagrin of the tower and other aircraft in the traffic pattern. A few minutes later, the OL-20 maintenance crew arrived to re-install the "pogies" so that I could finally taxi clear of the runway. The U-2 pilots were already envied for living in air-conditioned trailers at Bien Hoa, while all other aircrews lived in jalousied "hootches." This episode only increased the raucous flak that we endured at the bar.

Virtually all of my operational missions, except those from my final OL in South America, involved aerial photography. We performed the mission and stayed on course in those missions by using dead reckoning or navigating visually, simply looking down at the ground through the specialized cockpit drift sight. Of course, on long range deployments to and from the OLs, we often used the sextant for celestial navigation, using the upward-viewing mode in the same optical system.

The solitary and stressful mission environment demanded skillful individuals with unusual self-confidence and independence. Without exception, all of my squadron mates filled that bill. One of the unfortunate manifestations of that competence, however, was a certain prideful reluctance to openly share helpful information with one another. I felt so strongly about our failing in that regard that I wrote an article on the subject that was published in the December 1969 *SAC Combat Crew Magazine*. The article title was "There I Was!" and its main theme was that hangar flying, if conducted openly and responsibly, can contribute significantly to a unit's mission capability.

My last operational U-2 deployment was to Mendoza, Argentina. There, we established a two-airplane and three-pilot U-2 OL seeking to capture radioactive debris from French nuclear tests in the Pacific. The OL also had some large wing WB-57s from Kirtland AFB equipped for sampling, but they were maxed out at about 62,000 feet and did not accomplish any significant collection. After the intelligence folks had determined that a test detonation had occurred, the weather experts predicted when the debris cloud would be approaching the South

American continent. So, I got the nod to launch very late one night and climbed out in a northwesterly direction, passing over Mount Aconcagua, the highest mountain in the Andes. In a short while, I was over the Pacific Ocean, flying a preplanned sawtooth search pattern while keeping one eye on the cockpit instrument that would indicate the presence of radioactivity. After less than one hour, the indications were that I had, indeed, entered the debris cloud. I immediately initiated the appropriate procedures, so when I landed nearly three hours later, all of the airplane's sampling filters and high pressure bottles were full. Upon inspection, the airplane was found to have very high levels of radioactivity, but I suffered no ill effects.

It was shortly after my return from the Mendoza operation that we learned of the classified existence of a completely new and larger version of the U-2, referred to as the U-2R. The completely new design offered dramatically improved endurance and far safer, more forgiving flight characteristics at all altitudes than the older versions. Much to our delight, the new airplane had a far larger, modernized cockpit, a state-of-the-art ejection seat and—best of all—would permit use of a far more modern and comfortable *full* pressure suit, similar to what astronauts were using. All of the unit pilots were briefed on the new airplane and I was elated to learn that I would be among the first half dozen or so to check out in the U-2R.

That elation was tempered somewhat within a month or so by the news that I would be leaving the U-2 crew force. While I would continue in the U-2R checkout program and eventually accumulated nearly 60 hours in the airplane over ten flights in the US, I would not have the opportunity to fly that airplane operationally overseas. The reason was that I had been selected to manage and run the worldwide USAF U-2 operations as Chief of the U-2 Branch (DORSU) in the SAC Strategic Reconnaissance Center (SRC) located at SAC Headquarters in Offutt AFB, Omaha, Nebraska.

After every U-2 flight, a powerful feeling of euphoria would invariably follow, perhaps just from the relaxation of stress, but more probably from the natural feeling of having accomplished something worthwhile. Some of my squadron mates, I know, were able to feed on that feeling for days on end. In my case, however, I noticed that I would always have a restless feeling again the following day. It was as though I had come to realize that as exciting and fulfilling as flying the U-bird was, it was really only one step in my career and that even more important challenges lay in the future. It was that ambivalence that allowed me to overcome the disappointment of leaving the U-2 crew force when I did.

Although I scarcely appreciated the importance of the move at the time, it later proved to be one of the most important assignments in my Air Force career. Having the relatively low rank of major and being the only U-2-qualified officer in that headquarters provided me with invaluable staff experience and frequent contact with the top echelon of SAC leadership.

Ironically, despite the rigors and dangers inherent in U-2 operations, it was in a two place T-33 trainer at Davis-Monthan AFB that I had the most nearly fatal brush with the Grim Reaper during my entire 30-year flying career. It was on an extremely hazy days in Arizona, with severely restricted horizontal visibility. Vertical visibility was much better, however, so looking down at the airfield from above, I obtained permission from the tower for a simulated flameout (SFO) pattern to the active runway. That approach consisted of a single diving 360 degree turn that started at the "high key position" right over the field on the runway heading, turning 180 degrees and losing half of the altitude while proceeding to the "low key position" opposite the intended landing point, and then finally completing the 360 degree turn and pulling out of the dive near the runway end for the landing.

The potentially fatal situation was created by the fact that a twin-jet F-4C fighter bomber was on the Radar Approach Control (RAPCON) radio frequency performing a long straight-in radar-controlled approach to the same runway at the same time. Because the airfield control tower and RAPCON operators had failed to coordinate properly with each other, the tower's approval of my SFO pattern made a midair collision with the F-4C a near certainty. Thus, with severely restricted horizontal visibility, the F-4C was invisible to us in the descending T-33. After passing the "low key position," I continued in a constant diving left turn, looking at the runway to the left and concentrating on arriving at a point where a flameout landing would be possible. Just as I was rolling out on the runway heading and pulling the nose up to arrest our descent, the left side of the windscreen was suddenly filled with an F-4C with its landing gear and flaps down and the cockpit was simultaneously filled with the deafening roar of the F-4C's twin-jet exhausts. In that tiny fraction of a second, four individuals were given a new lease on life, since to have collided at that altitude would have inevitably caused both aircraft to crash.

So, all in all, as I prepared to leave for my new assignment, I felt that the unique professional credentials and insights gained from the U-2 experience had been worthwhile. But it was hard not to regret the difficult circumstances that the assignment had imposed on Ann and our family. The frequent and lengthy TDYs had made long range planning of family vacations impossible, and we sorely missed the close family and crew interactions that we had enjoyed in our tanker days. As before, Ann had uncomplainingly borne the burdens of loneliness, financial concerns and uncertainty, while continuing to be the loving mother and disciplinarian, too. But now it was time to move on.

Chapter Nine

MANAGING U-2 OPERATIONS

(FEBRUARY 1969-FEBRUARY 1971)

Months ago, having become established in the U-2 crew force, and being among the first few to qualify in the brand new U-2R, I was really "flying high." I therefore initially considered the news that I had been nominated to become director of the U-2 office (DORSU) at the Strategic Reconnaissance Center as something between an unwelcome illness and a full blown disaster. This chapter explains how that new assignment became a personal and professional blessing in disguise.

During the Cold War years and the war in Vietnam, the Air Force Strategic Air Command (SAC) operated and managed a wide variety of aerial vehicles tasked with collection of strategic intelligence in all parts of the world. Those vehicles included multiple versions of the RC-135s, high altitude U-2s, the triple-sonic SR-71, low altitude photographic drones (used only in Indochina), a other highly-classified vehicles that remain classified to this day. All of those vehicles and programs were managed and controlled at a central location, the Strategic Reconnaissance Center, or the "SRC," a highly-secure complex of rooms located in the basement of "H" Wing at Headquarters, SAC at Offutt AFB, Omaha, Nebraska.

Entry to the SRC complex was gained through cypher locks, and because of the highly-classified nature of the business conducted therein, rotating red ceiling lights were strategically placed to alert everyone whenever a "non-cleared" individual was in the area. Under those conditions, all maps had to be covered and conversations guarded to avoid any possible compromise of secret information. Twice each day—very early in the morning and in late afternoon—a formal centralized briefing was conducted by the SRC Director, in which staff officers representing each of the systems summarized their daily mission results, proposed new missions and briefed any other issues of importance. The pressure at those meetings was intense, because immediately afterward, the materials and matters discussed were taken directly to four-star General Bruce K. Holloway, Commander-in-Chief of SAC, and his senior staff.

So it was to this underground, windowless vault that I was now assigned, no longer to enjoy the adrenalin rush and exhilaration of flights at the edge of space, with their incredibly beautiful views of God's creation. Instead, I would be working entombed underground for six and a half days each week, with ten-hour days being the norm. But even before reporting for duty the first day, my family and I were to encounter a truly laughable series of incidents.

The four of us, traveling in our VW bug, arrived in Omaha one weekend in the dead of winter, with ice, snow and bitter cold a shock to our systems, accustomed as we were to the more hospitable Arizona weather. Actually, there were five of us, because our dachshund, Lucy, was also now a member of the family. Our first two nights were spent in a commercial motel not far from the base, as we awaited available temporary housing on base. Our accommodations consisted of two beds in a rather austere one room apartment with a small kitchenette tucked in one corner and a closet-like bathroom to the side. Warmth was provided by a strange radiator-like apparatus attached to some pipes protruding from the ceiling. That first night, we would periodically hear a pronounced clicking sound, followed by the whirring of the internal radiator fan, indicating that the thermostat had commanded the unit to turn on, providing heat. Unfortunately, the soft sound of the fan was immediately followed by a loud high-pitched metallic vibrating sound, much like a box of empty tin cans being roughly agitated.

The heater was distracting, but what came next was almost comical. Sometime in the wee hours of the first morning, we were awakened to feel a slight tremor in the entire room, followed by the unmistakable rumble and intermittent squeal of locomotive wheels slowly passing behind the motel. In the morning, I saw that the tracks were literally only six feet from the back of the building. That same day, we learned that if we could hold out one more day in the motel, temporary accommodations would be made available for us in one of the on base VIP quarters. The following day, we moved into a beautiful VIP cottage, only to find that the pipes were frozen! After another day of discomfort, the Base Civil Engineers resolved the situation and a few days later, we were able to receive assignment to our new permanent quarters, a very comfortable duplex in the Officers' Base Housing Area.

Ah, but ill fortune would strike again. My first full day at work in the SRC began on a dark and cloudy winter morning at 0700 hours. I parked the VW on a long circular drive designated for "Small Vehicle Parking" located right outside the entrance to "H" Wing, and entered the building. Ten hours later, after an exhausting first day on the job, I emerged from the building to find that the sun had gone down and nearly two feet of snow had fallen. Most of the other small cars on the circle had already been dug out and departed, but there was my VW bug, completely buried under a heavy accumulation of new snow.

Not yet having the proper snow removal tools, I put my briefcase on a pile of newly-plowed snow, and set to work using a loose leap binder to laboriously dig the car out from under its icy prison. As I was completing the job, finally getting to the windshield, I noticed a sheet of paper under the driver side windshield wiper. Welcome to Offutt AFB! I had not been on the base 48 hours, and had already received a parking ticket! I was to learn later that a special Small Car windshield sticker was required to legally park on the small car circle. Thankfully, when the circumstances of my recent arrival were explained later, the parking ticket was cancelled.

The U-2 branch manning consisted of two former U-2 pilots, that I had first met years ago in Buenos Aires, Roger Herman and Ed Smart, and a navigator, Fred Okimoto. A few weeks later, the manning was reduced to only two, when Roger and Ed departed.

The job of Chief, U-2 Branch (DORSU) consisted of two quite different, but closely-related functions. The first function was to be responsible for the actual planning, scheduling, executing, monitoring and reporting on every Air Force worldwide operational, non-training U-2 flight that was launched. That included flights from the several operating locations (OLs) that then existed in the continental US and overseas. Intelligence requirements came from intelligence agencies and were defined in terms of either point targets or coverage of designated areas, with weather and required frequency of coverage determining when flights were launched. The flight planning consisted of drawing the actual courses to be flown with sharp grease pencils on large, 4X5-foot aeronautical charts covered with clear plastic. The lengths of individual legs and frequency of turns all had to conform with guidelines designed to provide some measure of safety for the U-2 and complicate the task of anyone attempting to track or intercept it.

Since all of these flights were for the purpose of aerial photography, the takeoff times were established so that the aircraft would arrive over the first area of interest with the appropriate sun angle for high resolution photography. Once the entire route was drawn, the geographical coordinates of each turn point were noted and forwarded to the OL in a tasking/scheduling message. Then, several hours before launch, an execution message was sent, directing that the mission actually be flown. Immediately after the mission landed, we received comprehensive post-mission reports that were summarized and briefed up the chain. Occasional deviations which occurred from planned activities, of course, were immediately reported and acted upon.

Since we were performing these tasks for OLs in greatly separated locations as diverse as the continental US and Southeast Asia, those various functions were conducted at many different times throughout the day. When it was 7:00 AM in the morning at SRC, it was 9:00 PM at OL-20, our Southeast Asia base at Bien Hoa, South Vietnam. On the other hand, at about the time we would be going home from the SRC around 6:30 PM, it was a typical launch time of 8:30 AM at OL-20. For that reason, the round-the-clock functioning of the branch was unavoidable.

The twice-daily briefings provided a fascinating overall picture of worldwide strategic intelligence collection activities. At each meeting, highly-classified mission incidents and results were briefed by representatives of each system, and it was fascinating to say the least. That day to day exposure to the inside story of what was going on around the world was sorely missed two years later, after I left the SRC.

Over time, the advantages and disadvantages of the various collection vehicles were presented in stark contrast with each other. For example, the triple-sonic SR-71 was virtually immune from hostile threats in denied territory, but it could only be employed after a costly multi-airplane jet tanker task force had been deployed in the same operating theater to support it. Furthermore, its flight plans were computer-generated, requiring time-consuming "de-bugging" before use. U-2 missions could be planned and executed overnight, and were dramatically less costly.

Admittedly, the U-2 was far more vulnerable and could not compete with the SR-71 in heavily-defended areas. But the U-2 had some excellent defensive systems for many other situations and took higher resolution pictures. For those reasons, at times we felt that the SR-71 received the tasking over the U-2 solely to justify the high costs associated with its operation. Similar controversies occurred from time to time over the tasking of other competing intelligence gathering vehicles, as well.

I well remember one of the mild annoyances associated with planning U-2 operational missions. It was the frequency with which we would receive extremely short suspense new mission planning directives from the Joint Reconnaissance Center (JRC) located in Washington DC. Those short suspense taskings often required hours of work building up a completely new mission package, e.g. maps, flight plan, threat assessments, etc. Most frustrating of all was the fact that those short suspense requirements invariably would arrive *late on Friday afternoons*. It was as though the JRC staff spent their Friday afternoons over coffee, brainstorming exotic new uses for the U-2s, and then someone would say "Hey, let's see what the SRC can do with that!" before rushing off for their late Friday afternoon tee times. I can only think of one or two instances in which those late Friday "urgent" requirements eventually were validated and became actual missions.

The second, and in many ways the more important function inherent in the SRC assignment was to be the sole member of the SAC staff qualified to respond to any and all queries having to do with the U-2 weapon system. Moreover, my position on the SAC staff provided the U-2 unit at Davis-Monthan AFB with invaluable direct and timely access to the decision makers in Headquarters SAC. While performing this second function, I learned the secrets of staff coordination actions at all levels of a major headquarters, wrote multiple position papers on complex matters affecting the worldwide U-2 system, and had the opportunity to interact with and closely observe the leadership styles of a number of very senior Air Force officers.

Learning the process and art of obtaining staff concurrence on important issues, in particular, was an invaluable experience. Before any U-2-related directive or policy statement could be sent out by the headquarters, for example, it was my responsibility to obtain the concurrence of multiple staff agencies within the headquarters that might have an interest or be affected by the new directive. Similarly, when any issues were generated by other headquarters offices that might impact the U-2 program, it became my responsibility to understand them, take positions for or against, and staunchly defend my position. And to make it especially interesting, in most of those staffing interactions, I found myself interacting with officers who outranked me.

Another of the priceless benefits of the headquarters tour was the opportunity to interact closely with some very senior officers. Most were admirable role models and perfect gentlemen. I remember one, in particular, Major General Robert E. "Dutch" Huyser, who at the time was the SAC Chief of Plans. It fell to me to meet privately with him each week, to brief him on one particularly sensitive recurring U-2 mission that was not disclosed to the full SRC staff. During those meetings, we became fairly well acquainted with each other since our conversations often went beyond the business at hand. It was the same General Huyser who later became the US President's special envoy to the Shah of Iran before the fall. Ironically, fifteen years later, General Huyser and I would once again be working very closely together, when we were both working on tankers in international sales for the Boeing Company. It was a sad day when I learned of his death.

When I think back about the lessons learned from my tour at SRC, I think most often of one single episode that was instructive, as well as humbling. Very late one Friday afternoon, nearly everyone had left and

I was working alone on some project that needed to be completed before the following week. I heard the "buzz" of the cypher lock entry door and moments later the SRC Director, Colonel George Watson, came into my area and said, "Oh, Duke . . . . just who I wanted to see!" He then told me that he had just come from his regular Friday afternoon meeting with the entire SAC senior staff. During the meeting, he told me, he had overheard an offhand comment by General Holloway during a side conversation with two other general officers. General Holloway, it seems, had mumbled something like, "Well, I just wonder how busy the U-2 pilot is."

"So, Duke . . . see what you can come up with," said Colonel Watson. I thought the idea of preparing a formal briefing for General Holloway with such flimsy guidance and based on an offhand comment of his, to be absurd. To add that task to my existing workload seemed ridiculous. I am embarrassed to say that assessment came partially from the perception that Colonel Watson seemed at times to be pathetically eager to ingratiate himself to the SAC senior staff at the expense of the hard pressed SRC staff members. After stewing all weekend about what to do, I finally returned to my senses, gave it some serious thought, and built a briefing designed to accurately describe the details of the typical U-2 mission. This was before the days of overhead projectors and the like. All briefings were simply prepared by hand on large sheets of white paper, using magic markers. The five or six comprehensive charts that I came up with included graphics showing time, altitude, tasks, all organized in an easy to understand format.

After completing the charts and rehearsing the presentation multiple times until I felt comfortable with it, I put the charts into one of the large map drawers and forgot about it. Weeks went by and I was convinced that the briefing about "how busy the U-2 pilot is" had become a thing of the past. Three weeks later, however, after the regular Friday afternoon SRC briefing, Colonel Watson unexpectedly approached me and asked if I had prepared the briefing about the "U-2 pilot task saturation." I replied that I had, so he said "OK, get it and let's go!"

With the large briefing chart holder under my arm, the two of us walked rapidly up to the CINCSAC Command Section. Entering General Holloway's spacious office, we found the entire senior SAC staff, nearly a dozen general officers, with chairs facing a briefing easel at one end of the room. Colonel Watson explained the reason for the briefing, and I proceeded to make the presentation. Every officer in the room was a rated pilot, so the briefing generated a very lively discussion. In short, the meeting was an unqualified success, and I have always suspected that the positive exposure gained on that occasion played a part in my early "below-the-zone" promotion to lieutenant colonel about one year later.

Another positive aspect of the SRC assignment that I have not mentioned was that it included the opportunity to fly the North American T-39, twin-engine executive jet. The high performance of that airplane, with its shirtsleeve environment, range and ease of operation, made it ideal for multiple flights in a single day in support of the headquarters. Several days each month, therefore, I was able to forget the office for a few hours, launch in the morning, make several stops around the country, and often return early enough to pass by the office to check on things before going home. The airplane was an absolute joy to fly.

Despite the long working hours during our assignment in the SRC, life was good for the Woodhull family. No longer did we have to put up with repetitive TDYs away from home, so we were able to get into a fairly stable routine. It was during that time, too, that Chris and I greatly enjoyed some meaningful father-son activities in an activity known as the "YMCA Indian Guides." Young Ann was still at home with her Mom, and older brother Chris was enjoying himself at the Cardinal Spellman Catholic Elementary School. Our church home became St. Barnabas Episcopal Church where we were active. When the professional ice hockey season started, we began regularly attending games of the American Hockey League *Omaha Knights*.

That year, the *Knights* had a wonderfully successful year, winning the American Hockey League *Adams Cup*, the equivalent of the NHL *Stanley Cup*. Best of all, one of our favorite players on the *Knights'* team was called up to the *New York Rangers* in mid-season and was named the NHL Rookie of the Year. His last name was Fairbourn, very similar to Ann's maiden name, Fairburn. The association with the *New York Rangers* was pleasing to me, too, because I knew that many years before, my Father had played briefly for the *New York Rangers* until a serious knee injury ended his hockey career.

During our time there, we enjoyed Omaha's excellent restaurants, the horse races and other attractions of the Aksarben Festival, and antiquing in nearby Papillion. We socialized with other young couples and especially enjoyed our neighbors who lived in the other half of our duplex, Milvia and Barry Schmoyer. Barry was a staff officer in the aircraft maintenance field, and Milvia was a native-born Italian from Trieste who called me her "Viquingo," or "Viking." I am not sure why, but I always took that nickname as a compliment. Milvia and her other Italian girl friends were admired for actually making all sorts of pasta from scratch.

So, although life was good and the job satisfaction excellent, there was the realization that despite several 60-day TDY tours at OL-20, I had not yet completed a full year in Southeast Asia. At that stage in the Vietnam War, having that all-important year in Southeast Asia was absolutely essential for continued career progression. Early in our marriage, I had always thought of an unaccompanied overseas assignment as something to be avoided at all costs. But ever since Ann and I had decided on a full career in the Air Force, that wider perspective caused us to appreciate the unavoidable necessity of making sacrifices for longer term benefits.

Some months prior to the two-year anniversary of my SRC assignment, I had become aware of a SAC policy established in June 1969 that allowed volunteers to Southeast Asia to be reassigned out of the headquarters at the end of only two years, instead of the usual three years. Fearing the adverse career impact of my lack of a year in Southeast Asia, I prepared a detailed request for release after two years, including comprehensive justification for the request and a complete plan for obtaining my replacement. Some weeks later, I was gratified to receive notification that my application had been approved, and I would be departing in January 1971.

It was at about this time that young Ann took it upon herself to send a letter to the White House informing the president of our relocation to a new home. Each time she did so over the next several years, she always received a cordial letter from the White House staff with thanks for keeping them informed.

Chapter Ten

THAILAND TOUR

After two personally fulfilling and productive years as Chief, U-2 Branch in the Strategic Reconnaissance Center, I was on my way to that dreaded one-year unaccompanied tour overseas. After we located and rented a house in Winter Park, Florida near Ann's parents' home in Orlando, she prepared to settle down to wait out the lonely year with our two children, now six and twelve, respectively. After a few days of leave setting up housekeeping, we said goodbye and I headed for my new assignment in the Special Missions Division of SAC's 307th Strategic Wing at the U-Tapao Royal Thai Navy Base near Sattahip, Thailand.

During the period 1966-1975, U-Tapao was maintained as the single most important base for launching and recovering B-52 bombers and KC-135 tankers supporting the Vietnam War effort. Prior to 1965, the heavy bombers had operated from more distant bases in Guam and Okinawa, but because of the distances involved, those missions required long mission times and aerial refueling support. Tankers had also been supporting tactical fighters in Vietnam, operating from Kadena AB, Okinawa. But again, the distances involved greatly reduced the flexibility and operational effectiveness of that support.

Stationing the B-52s in Thailand at U-Tapao completely eliminated their need for aerial refueling support. And movement of the KC-135 *Young Tiger Tanker Task Force* from Kadena AB to U-Tapao dramatically improved the timeliness of support and increased fuel offloads available to tactical fighters in Vietnam and Thailand.

Upon arrival at U-Tapao on a chartered commercial airliner, I reported in to the Special Missions Division of the 307th Strategic Wing, a four-man office that was charged with a wide variety of mission support responsibilities and special projects. All of the bomber and tanker aircrews at U-Tapao were serving tours of duty of 60-90 days' duration away from their home units in the US. The 307th Strategic Wing, therefore, was the unit that became their overseas home unit and maintained the infrastructure to support them.

Before any aircrew arriving at U-Tapao could be cleared to fly an operational mission, they were required to be certified as having completed a comprehensive day-long orientation process covering everything from mundane logistical matters to the very specific parameters and rules of engagement related to the missions that they were about to undertake. Managing and maintaining that orientation program was one of the Special Mission Division's primary responsibilities, and I became one of its primary briefers, specializing in air traffic control matters.

The intense operations tempo of the wing meant that a large number of USAF bomber and tanker sorties were constantly moving through Thai airspace, constituting a substantial midair collision hazard for the numerous civilian airliners transiting the area. For that reason, strictly-defined airspace and altitude reservations had been negotiated with the Thai air traffic control agencies. Specifically, all flights departing from and returning to U-Tapao were required to adhere to very strict course and altitude restrictions amounting to imaginary tunnels of authorized airspace in the sky. My continuing task was to ensure that the crews fully understood those requirements and that they adhered to them, and to investigate and report on those inevitable occasions when for various reasons those requirements had been violated. A very pleasurable aspect of that job was to be the designated USAF Liaison Officer to Bangkok Center, the controlling air traffic control agency in Thailand. So, each month I spent two days alone in Bangkok meeting with the Bangkok Center staff, addressing air traffic problems and smoothing relationships.

Working virtually seven days a week was a blessing, since it minimized distractions and made the days pass quickly. My daily routine did not vary much from day to day. Each day before the heat of the day, I would be up early and go for a three mile run, return for a shower, walk one block to the Officers' Club Mess Hall for breakfast, return to the barracks to pick-up the used bicycle that I had acquired for onbase transportation, and proceed to work in the 307th SW headquarters building, usually arriving before 0800 hours. Updating and conducting bomber and tanker crew briefings which were held nearly every weekday, occupied most mornings. At noon, I would return to my quarters, go for another run, shower, eat a light lunch in the room, and return to work.

After work, I would bicycle home, shower, and, if time permitted before supper, start writing letters, work on correspondence courses or read. After the sun went down and things cooled off somewhat, I would walk to the Officers' Club and almost invariably order the very same meal every night: "Kow Pot," fried rice with either chicken or shrimp, topped with a fried egg. The waitresses were all young Thai girls who spoke little or no English. One of their expressions that I do recall frequently hearing was "No Hab!" after being asked for something not available. After supper, I would return to the room to finish my daily letter to Ann, read and turn in.

My home away from home was a large, three-story concrete structure with small one-man air-conditioned rooms, each of which opened out onto an outside open air corridor running the length of the building. Each floor had a large gang latrine at one end of the building. Each individual room had a bed, table, lamp, steel locker, fluorescent ceiling lights, a small refrigerator, and an in-the-wall air conditioner. The large gang latrines had high ceilings so that when taking a shower, you could always look up and see a dozen or so 8"-long, greenish-yellow geckos stuck to the ceiling, enjoying the warm, moist atmosphere. After a while, you became accustomed to their swivel-headed stares, and hearing their two-syllable, sibilant chirps. The building also had one rather unique added feature: a troop of washer ladies who spent every day in the yard beside the building, providing free lance laundry service for the residents.

The intensive KC-135 tanker activity at U-Tapao was carried-out independently of the B-52 operations. Operating under the control of the

Young Tiger Tanker Operations Center, multiple tanker sorties flew day and night to provide refueling support to tactical fighter operations over Vietnam and Laos. To provide that support, a number of racetrack-shaped tanker orbits known as "anchors" had been established. Referred to by color, e.g. "Orange Anchor" or "Red Anchor," they were maintained outside of high threat areas over Thailand and generally north and west of the Thai-Laos border area. Tankers loitered along the oval "racetrack" patterns, awaiting combat aircraft on their way to and from targets in North Vietnam and Laos.

Because of my status as a former KC-135 instructor pilot and because of the frequency of tanker sorties flying out of U-Tapao, it was easy for me to maintain my credibility with the tanker crews by flying with them several times each month. Unfortunately, there was no need or provision made for my regaining currency in the '135, so all of my flying at U-Tapao was of the "sandbag" variety. That was not as satisfying as flying the airplane, but enjoyable, all the same. Often, during actual refueling contacts, I would go back to the boom operator's compartment and look directly down on the receiver pilots as they took on fuel. I always felt a strange sense of camaraderie with them since two or three years before, I had been the one that was heading north into unfriendly skies.

All of my flying at U-Tapao, with one exception, was in the tankers. On one memorable occasion, however, I did fly with a crew on a single B-52 bombing mission attacking the Ho Chi Minh Trail. Seated in the bowels of the airplane behind the main flight crew, I was not able to see much, so contented myself with simply monitoring the interphone to know what was going on. Because I was rather fatigued from the long hours that I had been working, I even dozed a bit in the early part of the flight. That fact did not escape the notice of one of the other crew members, who made a snide remark about it to his buddies on the interphone.

When the "bombs away" moment came, I felt a sudden rippling vibration as each of the 105 individual bombs rapidly departed the airplane. At the same time, the dramatic reduction in the weight of the airplane resulted in a very perceptible lifting sensation of the airplane. After we landed, the crew presented me with one of their elaborate colorful unit patches worn proudly on their flight suits to show the world how many B-52 combat sorties they had flown. Of course, in my case, the patch had only a single digit . . . the number "1."

It was nearly three weeks after arriving at U-Tapao that I received my first letter from Ann. In fact, I received my first six letters at that time, all at once. And that was the way her letters usually arrived, i.e. in small batches of two or three at a time. In the days before the internet, e-mail and Skype, simple hand-written letters were the only way we could communicate with one another across the many miles. Today, we call it "snail mail." And it was just that lack of contact, that sense of isolation and loneliness and of being so far from her and our children on the other side of the world that had caused me to dread and to fear the assignment.

But a strange thing happened. As we got into the routine of writing daily letters to each other, the flow of ideas and understanding between us grew in a way that was incredibly calming and reassuring. As strange as it may seem, in some ways we communicated with each better during that time, than at some other times when we were together again. No matter how long you live with someone, you can never stop trying to communicate honestly and openly with each other. It is the key to a happy marriage, and Ann has always been better at it than I.

Ann's letters were full of encouraging news about Annie and Chris in school, her folks and other family members in the Orlando area, and how she was keeping busy. She had joined one of the military Waiting Wives groups, in which other wives in her situation could exchange information and suggestions. Sadly, during the Vietnam War, the general public was not at all supportive of the wives of servicemen. After she experienced several instances of actual hostility from individuals who had learned that I was overseas and involved in the war, Ann no longer would even tell people what her husband did. That situation is a sad chapter in our national life.

In June 1971, after six months at U-Tapao, I was able to take a two week leave and get a ride all the way back to Orlando, Florida on a KC-135 that was returning to its home unit at McCoy AFB. It was during that visit and while I was driving home from a movie with our daughter, Annie, that I experienced a kidney stone attack for the first time in my life. That experience, and the other kidney stone attacks that I have subsequently suffered, have given me an deep appreciation for the pain of childbirth experienced by the women of the world.

I learned later that the attack was caused by all that jogging in the hot Southeast Asian sun and failing to drink sufficient quantities of water. Anyway, it was wonderful seeing how capably Ann was managing everything, but the visit was all too short. On the return commercial flight enroute to the west coast to catch a military flight back to Thailand, American Airlines was kind enough to upgrade me to First Class, where Jeannie Pruett, the country music star, was my traveling companion.

After returning to U-Tapao, three salutary events took place before my tour ended. The first was an insignificant incident, but one that I remember fondly. Upon returning to the barracks for lunch one day, I noticed a commotion surrounding the group of washer ladies on the lawn at the side of the barracks. One of the ladies was lying on the ground at the side of a large puddle of water, crying. One of her English-speaking companions reported that she had been bitten by a "habu," meaning a venomous snake. She was sure she was going to die. All I could think of doing was to get her to the hospital right away, so I swooped up all 85 pounds of her into my arms, got on my bike, and pedaled the several blocks to the emergency room. The medics could find no evidence of a snakebite and she didn't die. No one ever located the snake so we don't even know if she had been bitten, but from then on, all of the washer ladies treated me with exaggerated respect.

The second event was my completely unanticipated early promotion to the rank of lieutenant colonel. My year group of majors was due to enter the primary zone for promotion consideration to lieutenant colonel after the end of my tour in Thailand. When promotion lists were customarily released, they always listed the Primary Zone names, but then included individuals who had been promoted "below the zone," or one or two years early. So when the promotion list for the year group ahead of me came out in August 1971, I had little interest in it and absolutely no expectation of appearing on the "below the zone" list. But that, in fact, is what happened. Greatly surprised, but certainly gratified beyond belief, I arranged to send Ann a commercial telegram announcing the good news. Unfortunately, that priceless little piece of family history was lost and was never seen again. Because of the Officer Grade Limitation Act, the actual pinning-on of the new rank would have to wait nearly a year, but as a confirmed "LC" selectee, my status in the world and at work had certainly been enhanced.

Finally, the third event had far greater immediate impact on our family. Prior to departing SRC for the Thailand assignment, I had submitted a formal application for a security assistance job at one of the US Military Groups in Latin America. Those assignments were appealing because they would include the family, involved learning another language, and would give me a chance to return to South America where I had previously spent time. I had scored well on the Air Force Language Aptitude Test, but had only a fond hope of receiving one of those coveted assignment.

Much to my pleasure and surprise, however, I was called one day to the Personnel Office and notified that I had been selected for assignment to the US Military Group located in Rio de Janeiro, Brazil. The icing on the cake was the proviso that my 12-month tour in Thailand would be reduced by nearly two months, so that I could begin the Portuguese language course with a new class at the Defense Language Institute-West Coast.

So once again, destiny had smiled on us, and very soon we would be on our way to a new adventure. And it truly turned out to be a life-changing experience.

Chapter Eleven

BRAZIL

(January 1972-June 1975)

I have always said that one of the most satisfying benefits of my 30-year Air Force career was having the opportunity to learn the Portuguese language and then to enter the Brazilian culture, living and working virtually as a member of the Brazilian Air Force (Força Aérea Brasileira/FAB) for over three years, and beyond. In fact, those factors were responsible for the two careers that I subsequently enjoyed—with the Boeing Airplane Company, and later with private industry after I left the Air Force in 1985. This chapter reports on our language training at the Defense Language Institute-West Coast (DLI-WC), and the three wonderful years in which I worked in the Brazilian Air Ministry and we enjoyed some wonderful family times in the beautiful and glamorous city of Rio de Janeiro.

After receiving the very welcome news of our new assignment in Brazil, we immediately made plans for the long trip across the country from Florida to the Presidio of Monterey, California, to begin Portuguese language training.

As soon as I was able to return home, we packed up the VW and launched ourselves into another adventure. The area around Monterey and Carmel Valley, California where the kids were soon in an Episcopal school, has to be one of the most beautiful in the country. We were lucky to quickly find and rent a very nice bungalow in Pacific Grove, not far from the Presidio of Monterey, where we would be in class each day. I said "we" would be in class, because during the in-processing we learned that Ann had been approved to take the full Portuguese course right along with me on a "space available" basis, and that is exactly what she did.

The rationale for allowing selected dependents to accompany the spouses in the language training was simply that experience has shown that when both are fluent in the language, a more productive and happy overseas assignment results. Of course, during our time at DLI, there were many Sunday evenings in which Ann would half-heartedly protest that she didn't have to go to school the next day . . . but she always did.

The DLI basic Portuguese course was six months long, with the ultimate objective of achieving a "3-3" ("Superior") speaking and comprehension level on the Defense Language Proficiency Test (DLPT). The DLI Portuguese Department consisted of seven native speaking professors, of whom six were Brazilian and one, Mr. Tavares, was from the Azores and who spoke with an accent that varied somewhat from the others. He was a typically humble, soft spoken Portuguese man who was constantly the object of gentle ribbing from the more assertive Brazilians.

Mr. Tavares, however, was a gifted joke teller who masterfully held his own through wonderful stories that always reflected poorly on the general intelligence of Brazilians. We had a total of twelve students in our class, with individuals representing all services. Three of the other students eventually served in Brazil with us and became fast friends. One couple, Gayle and Linda Morris, had two daughters who became close friends with our children. And David Rogus, a US Naval officer on his way to teach English in the Brazilian Naval Academy, eventually met and married an American school teacher in Rio, and went on to a successful career in the US State Department.

To oversimplify, the basic DLI teaching methodology consisted of memorizing short 12-15 line Portuguese dialogues for each lesson every night. The topics could be anything from shopping for shoes, filling a prescription at a drugstore, or looking for an apartment. The first class activity each morning was always for the students to take turns reciting the dialogues, which were then manipulated by the professors by changing the verb tenses and substituting words to the phrases so that new meanings could be produced from the same basic sentence structures. It was amazing how those structures would stick in your mind. There was heavy emphasis on conversation between students and professors, with little or no English spoken at all, except during occasional hours when complex grammatical concepts and rules were taught.

We played children's games, learned and sang songs, had regular reading assignments, listened to Voice of America tapes, and day after day performed the laborious task of memorizing and reciting the daily dialogues. The methods used may sound unorthodox, but they were undeniably very effective because before long most in the class, to varying degrees, had gained some ability to speak, read and understand the language. And at the end of the course, most of the students attained at least the "2-2" ("Intermediate-High") rating in the DLPT, and three of us achieved the coveted "3-3" ("Superior") capability level.

In short, language school was challenging, stimulating and entertaining. The final examination for each student consisted of making a formal 40-minute oral presentation in Portuguese on his or her subject of choice, followed by conducting a 15-minute question and answer session with the faculty members. In Ann's very successful final presentation, she offered herself as a candidate for the US presidency, using the campaign slogan "Tio Sam Precisa de uma Mulher" (Uncle Sam Needs a Woman). Before she gave her talk, she had tipped-off Dona Dira, the only female professor, of her intent. When Ann announced her campaign slogan during the talk, Dona Dira stood, clapped and cheered. All but one of the male professors only smiled and derisively shook their heads. The one exception, Mr. Warren, defended Ann vociferously, even taking time out of the Q&A to reprimand his chauvinistic colleagues for their bad manners.

My final exam presentation, by comparison, was a rather mundane talk entitled "Aviação para o Leigo" (Aviation for the Layman), about airplanes and the principles of flight. Shortly afterwards, I was informed that I was one of five students among all DLI-WC students in the entire school selected as candidates to receive the Association of the US Army Achievement Plaque as outstanding student of the year. The final selection would be determined by submission of an essay entitled "The Importance to Military Personnel of Learning a Foreign Language." The original essay that I submitted resulted in my selection for the award. The following is an excerpt from that essay:

> "... Undertaking the intensive study of a foreign language is indeed a rare and valuable privilege. Only one who has actually experienced the trials and rigorous discipline of such an experience can fully appreciate the sense of fulfillment that comes from developing some degree of competence in a foreign language. But for members of the Armed Forces today, there are far more important reasons for studying a foreign language than the mere personal benefits that may be derived .... in the context of a troubled world torn by distrust, misunderstanding and suspicion, it is clear that lasting world peace depends as much on expansion of human understanding and cooperation, as it does on the military deterrence of aggressive acts ..."

After a brief leave to visit with Ann's parents in Florida and a few days after my 38th birthday, we made our way via commercial air to Rio de Janeiro, Brazil. We were met at the airport by the family that we would be replacing, and they escorted us to the "Clube Militar," a large facility for Brazilian officers' and their families who needed temporary lodging. That would be our home for several weeks.

The day after our arrival, we were completely on our own. While the kids visited with new friends, Ann and I immediately went to work looking through real estate ads in local papers, visiting neighborhoods and inquiring of the ever-present "porteiros," men who were always available at the front of apartment buildings, whether or not there might be available apartments in their building. It was at that time that the conversations of DLI Lesson #4, "Procurando um Apartamento" (Getting an Apartment) came to life in a gratifyingly vivid way. It was literally as though we had done it all before.

Very soon we had our choices narrowed down to two, both in the Leblon neighborhood, and after a weekend of debating the pros and cons, made our decision. It was an apartment that fully occupied the second floor of a seven story apartment building on a picturesque ascending cobblestone street with relatively few homes, located at the extreme west end of Leblon, at Rua Sambaiba, 254.

Shortly after deciding on our new home, the grapevine provided us with a strong recommendation for an available live-in cook and maid. Although she spoke no English, Jandira had a very appealing and quiet personality, was a terrific cook, and very soon became an important and valued member of our household. She lived with us in a small area off the kitchen. She and our young daughter, Annie, were fast friends and I attribute the fluency that Annie gained in the language largely to the evenings that she spent visiting with Jandira and watching soap operas on local TV.

The US military had a very low profile in Rio. The American organizational entity in Rio was called the Joint US-Brazil Military Commission (JBUSMC) and each US service had its own small office located in the corresponding service's headquarters. With the basic mission of managing security assistance programs for the Brazilian Air Force (Força Aérea Brasileira/FAB), the Air Force Section was located in a corner of the fourth floor of the Brazilian Air Ministry in downtown Rio. Our manning consisted of five officers, three sergeants and three Foreign Nationals, e.g. two secretaries and a jack-of-all-trades "despachante" who ran errands and worked wonders cutting the inevitable bureaucratic red tape in various commercial and government offices.

Our office kept a twin-engine Convair C-131 aircraft at the nearby Santos Dumont Airport, to provide transportation around the country for ourselves and the US Navy admiral who was Chief of the US Navy Section. Midway through our tour in Rio, Admiral Thor Hansen, a former Rhodes Scholar and US Naval Academy graduate, assumed that position. Because his mother, Lillian, had been our son's first grade teacher in Tucson, Arizona years before, we had instant rapport with him and I effectively became his personal pilot.

On one memorable flight with Admiral Hanson and his official party, moments after taking off from *Val de Cães* airport in Belem, Brazil, the starboard engine suddenly failed ("blew a jug"), necessitating an immediate return and emergency landing relying on the remaining single engine. That airfield was the same one at which I had made an SC-54 night time engine out landing more than ten years before.

Upon arrival, I learned that I was now the Chief of the Training and Personnel Division of the JBUSMC Air Force Section. That "division," of course, consisted of one person: me. As such, I personally had an $850,000 annual Military Assistance Program (MAP) budget to develop and manage. To accomplish that task, I had to understand and assess the needs of every unit in the FAB, and become intimately familiar with all of their technical and professional schools throughout the country. For that reason, having our own airplane to facilitate visits throughout the country was essential. In addition, since Brazil had just recently purchased a squadron of modern F-5E fighters from the US to be delivered in less than three years, a massive training effort would be required to establish the self-sustaining infrastructure for them to receive, maintain and safely operate them. Of all of my responsibilities in Brazil, I found the annual preparation and submission of that $850,000 annual budget to be the most difficult.

The training that I was able to offer varied widely. Courses in an infinite variety of subjects were available in US Air Force technical schools in the United States, but proficiency in English was required. The candidates therefore usually had to be identified and prepared well in advance. On several occasions, I arranged for visits of Mobile Training Teams (MTTs) to come to Brazil, to present short courses or workshops to selected FAB audiences. In many of those cases, I personally became the facilitating interpreter. Those training visits were especially taxing, since they involved arranging and monitoring lodging and ground transportation for the visitors over and above the actual training activities. And during one 18-month period, I lead a seminar group of five senior FAB officers taking the USAF Air War College off campus course.

Preparing FAB for the operational incorporation of the soon-to-be-delivered F-5E fighters brought me into close contact with the illustrious FAB First Fighter Group at Santa Cruz AB, not far from Rio. That organization had served with distinction during WWII in Italy, flying its own P-47 fighters against the Germans. More importantly,

F-5E preparations provided me frequent contact with that unit's commander, then-colonel Lauro Ney Menezes. Colonel Menezes was an already legendary figure and a prolific writer and thinker on national security issues who was later was to hold significant higher offices, finally retiring as a major brigadeiro. With his capable and enthusiastic leadership and support, during my tour in Brazil we were able to qualify the first cadre of F-5E pilots, establish an autonomous in-country maintenance and training facility at Santa Cruz AB, and successfully receive the initial flights of F-5Es in Brazil.

The years that we lived in Brazil coincided with the government administration headed by former Army general Emílio Médici. Médici's government was the third military government to be in charge since the Armed Forces 1964 coup d'état that deposed President João Goulart, who openly supported the Communist Bloc. In typically Brazilian fashion, that event had been virtually bloodless—"the revolution of perfume and roses"—and from our perspective as ordinary citizens on the ground eight years later, the military government seemed rather benign and not at all in evidence. Political freedoms were unquestionably restrained by the regime, but the policies and actions of the government were not even remotely similar to those of truly repressive regimes such as Argentina and Peru.

To be sure, the economy had its ups and downs. Twice during our time in Rio, the national currency was completely revamped. Initially, we used *cruzeiros* as the medium of exchange. Over time, when inflation progressed so that we were all commonly carrying *cruzeiros* with face values in the thousands, the Government took decisive action by devaluing the currency overnight. One morning we woke up to learn that we could all just "ignore" the three zeroes, until some new bills could be printed. Another manifestation of the economic instability was the fact that our civilian apartment monthly rent was not stated as a fixed monetary amount. Instead, our rent was stated as a multiple of the national minimum hourly wage rate, or "salário mínimo." For that reason, as the official hourly minimum wage rate went up every few months, so did our rent!

For our family, living in Rio in the early 1970s was a wonderfully enriching and enjoyable experience. "Cariocas," the term applied to residents of Rio, are famously fun-loving, with a cheerful and positive viewpoint about life. Paradoxically, most individuals with whom we had contact exhibited a strong work ethic, as well. As a result, we had very little difficulty making friends and adapting to the local culture. Friendships that we formed in those years have lasted decades, and we have been visited multiple times in the US by our Brazilian friends and their offspring. We have come to think of Brazil as our second home.

If a hostile nation were ever to invade Brazil, success would be almost guaranteed if the invasion were to be launched during the annual four-day pre-Lenten Carnaval festival. During that event, the country devotes itself totally to either partying or simply getting away from the large cities for a mini-vacation with the family. For the revelers, the last night always consists of a memorable all-night parade of samba clubs attended by thousands.

Another uniquely-Brazilian annual event that we always attended was New Years' Eve on Leblon Beach. It was there that exotic Black priestesses from Bahia in their long white lace dresses offered their special blessings of the old African *macumba* folk religion. Each of the priestesses would stand in the dark on the sand puffing on a large black cigar, surrounded by a circle of interested onlookers. When someone indicated a willingness to part with a few *cruzeiro* notes in exchange for a blessing, the priestess would take a drag on her cigar and blow its "purifying" smoke on that person, accompanying that action with some unintelligible incantations. For an extra fee, she would put a small paper boat with a candle in the surf for you, symbolizing the banishment of all one's troubles. Very few enlightened Brazilians actually believe in the powers of *macumba*, but they flock to the Leblon Beach anyway for the fun of it, or in the hope that the mysterious magical blessing will actually work.

Life in Rio was never dull, constantly providing opportunities for new experiences. On one occasion, when Ann expressed more than casual curiosity about the *macumba* religion and rituals to a Brazilian friend, we soon received a once-in-lifetime invitation.

Very late a few nights later, we found ourselves in the dark, climbing up a steep and narrow winding path on a jungle-covered mountain overlooking the city lights of Rio, far below. With our friend in the lead, we had passed through a *favela*, or slum area initially, and were now passing dense low bushes, making our way higher and higher through the muggy, silent night. Several times we were passed closely in the dark by indistinct silent figures descending along the path. Finally, after close to an hour, we became aware of the barely perceptible sound of muffled beating drums. The drum beat increased in strength as we climbed, and before long, a low building and dimly-lit doorway came into view.

When we entered the building, we were amazed to see that it was actually a very small amphitheater, crowded with 40-50 men and women, all wearing white. We had entered at the level of the top tier, and moments after we entered, we were unsettled to see that most of those present turned to look in our direction. Our friend tried to tell us something like " . . . não se preocupem, eles sabem que vocês estão comigo" / "don't worry, they know you are with me." The only illumination in the room came from rows of candles, and together with the crowd, they created waves of oppressive heat and smoke.

Down below, in the center of the room were men playing the drums, accompanying a number of Black Bahian priestesses swaying in a dance-like trance, wearing the accustomed long white lace gown, and smoking large black cigars. The noise was deafening and conversation was impossible. One of the priestesses came up to our level in the room and gave us each a brief blessing of cigar smoke, but no words were passed. After observing the scene a few more minutes, we felt it best not to overstay our welcome, so we made our way outside. We had not learned a great deal about the *macumba* religion that night, but we certainly had enjoyed seeing the fascinating spectacle. Sadly, the dangerous security situation and common presence of drug gangs in *favelas* nowadays, would make such an adventure impossible.

A second memorable incident in Brazil will forever be remembered in our family as the famous "orange episode." Late one evening, Ann came to me in the back bedroom and breathlessly exclaimed: "Duke, go up front and look across the street! Someone is getting ready to burglarize the house!" We had very large, open windows in the front of our apartment, so I got up and moved slowly in the dark to a point in the apartment where I could look out and see the scene below.

Sure enough! The house across the street was surrounded by a wall, and a mysterious figure was lurking near the recessed doorway leading onto the property! Whenever a passing car's headlights would shine in his vicinity, he would skulk in the shadows so as not to be seen. Living on the floor right above us in our apartment building were Jim and Zee Moyer. Jim was an Air Force lieutenant colonel and also an office mate of mine in the Air Force Section.

Quickly, I went to the phone, called Jim and asked him if he had a flashlight. Learning that he did, I gave him my plan: "Jim, let's hang up and count to twenty. At "20," turn your flashlight beam on him. I have a bowl of oranges on the table near the front window, so I'll heave one at him!" We executed the plan perfectly. Picking up two oranges, I waited. When the count got to twenty, I saw the light beam come on, revealing the burglar, so I immediately threw an orange, hoping to at least scare him away. Miraculously, the orange arced across the street in the dark and came down, hitting him on the shoulder. He immediately took off, running desperately up the ascending cobblestones until he was out of sight. Jim called us almost immediately, and we congratulated ourselves on having done our civic duty.

The next morning, as Jim and I descended to the sidewalk to await our ride to work, João the porteiro, approached me and asked me if I knew "what had happened." Having no idea what he was talking about, I told him so. He then informed me that his cousin had been hired by the family across the street to watch their house while they were away on vacation . . . . and that last night, he had been viciously attacked! Jim and I immediately gave him doleful looks and, shaking our heads, expressed outrage at how dangerous the streets had become.

Both of our children attended the *Escola Americana*, an institution whose student body was 65% Brazilian, with many other nationalities making up the rest. The common language of the school was nominally English, but classes in the Portuguese language and Brazilian history were mandatory, and the language of the school yard was largely Portuguese. Located among the tall jungle trees on the hills of Gávea, the western-most suburb of the city, the school was an attractive white building with red tile roofs, high ceilings and tall open air windows allowing the shade and breezes to cool the classrooms. Long-tailed marmoset monkeys could often be seen, sitting on the classroom window sills, eying the students and being eyed in return.

The academics at EA were excellent. Our daughter, in particular, developed such a strong affinity for mathematics that she was able years later to breeze through college level math courses and earn a degree in electrical engineering. Our son, Chris, six years older than his sister, thoroughly enjoyed life on the beach and soccer, or "futebol" as it is known there. On one occasion, Chris and I saw the world famous Pelé play with his home team, Santos, against our favorite Rio team, Botafogo. Pelé, of course, was already famous for being the star of the national team that had won Brazil's third World Cup title in 1970 in Mexico. At this writing, they have won four more World Cup titles. While Chris had only average soccer skills for a Brazilian, because of the moves he had acquired in Brazil, he was considered to be incredibly skillful later in high school, back in the US.

Ann thrived in Rio, enjoying having live-in help, driving herself everywhere in the city, learning about Brazilian folk art and culture, and often escorting Brazilian lady friends on day trips. As a former teacher, for a time she taught the second grade at the Irish School, a small private school in our neighborhood. We entertained Brazilian Air Force couples often, and Ann was famous for gently insisting that the men and women intermingle at our parties, instead of following the usual Brazilian custom of spending the time at opposite ends of the room, either talking about babies or airplanes.

On one memorable occasion, she was being escorted alone on a visit to the central Brazilian Air Force Hospital in Rio by its commander. After touring the facilities for over an hour, they were seated in the cafeteria at the lunch hour, when he asked her, "Mrs. Woodhull, what do you think of our hospital?" Thinking that he was referring to the lunchroom, she had intended to say that it was rather noisy, or "barulento." That would have been an acceptable response. Instead, she used the word "bagunça," which translates roughly to a "hopelessly confused and disorganized mess." They both had a good laugh over that.

We all experienced moments of embarrassment from time to time caused by our less-than-perfect command of the language. On my very first trip away from Rio early in my tour, one of our sergeants and I visited a supply depot in São Paulo commanded by a very senior officer. The day had gone perfectly, and during our final conversation, the commander mentioned that he wanted to ask one final important question dealing with personnel classifications in our air force. As luck would have it, the sergeant who had accompanied me on the visit just happened to be an expert in that field. So, I responded by saying, "Brigadeiro, thank-you for your question. With your permission, I would like Sergeant Alonzo here to give you an answer, because he is an expert in that field." When the brigadeiro burst our laughing, I knew something was wrong. By confusing two fairly similar words, "perito" and "perdido," I had told the brigadeiro that I wanted Sergeant Alonzo to answer the question because, on that subject, he was totally confused.

Sometimes, a single letter can get you into trouble. On one occasion, my wife and son obtained a "hop" on a Brazilian Air Force plane to do a little sightseeing in Buenos Aires, Argentina. Ann had always dreamed of seeing a traditional Argentine tango with the violins, guitars and concertinas, complete with macho male in his suit and fedora, dancing with a beautiful señorita in black dress, heels and a rose in her hair. After getting in a taxi in Buenos Aires, Ann addressed the driver in Portuguese: "We want to see a tanga show!" The driver, hesitated for a moment, then looked back at her and asked in Spanish: "How old's the kid?" She responded that he was fifteen, so with a shrug from the driver, they were off. A few minutes later, they arrived in the front of a garishly-lighted strip club, complete with ten foot high pictures of scantily clad female dancers. It was immediately apparent that a mistake had been made, so Ann announced "I am his mother! Take us back to the hotel!" The reason for the mix up was that the word "tanga" in both Portuguese and Spanish means "string bikini." Ann didn't get to see a real tango show until several years later.

During my tour in Brazil, I was made to truly feel a part of the Brazilian Air Force. I flew with them, attended staff meetings, and was welcomed in all of their technical and professional schools. The identification card provided to me was identical to that of any FAB flying officer, with no indication whatever of my foreign nationality. One exceptional gesture especially gratifying to me was having the senior FAB general in charge of personnel and training asked me to pre-screen and report to him on all foreign vendor sales presentations before they were referred to the FAB Air Staff.

* * *

There are two key indicators of success or failure in any military career. The first, of course, is whether or not one is promoted in rank when he becomes eligible in the primary zone, or better yet, early "below the zone." The second important indicator is whether or not he is selected to attend one of the professional service schools in residence. For the Air Force, the senior service school is Air War College (AWC), a one-year course of study for lieutenant colonels or full colonels in residence at Air University at Maxwell AFB, Montgomery, Alabama. Nearly three months prior to the end of our three-year assignment in Rio, we learned that my name had appeared on the schools list, thus informing us of our next destination after Brazil.

Chapter Twelve

AIR WAR COLLEGE

(JUNE 1975-JULY 1976)

Returning to the United States, I became a member of the "Bicentennial Class of 1976" of the Air Force senior service school, the Air War College. Although by no means a guarantee, that assignment boded well for my eventually achieving a promotion to full colonel. But of equal importance, since I would be excused from flying for the year, the assignment offered our family an opportunity to establish some semblance of a normal domestic routine, without the constant travel, separations and periodic crises of my previous assignments.

Located at Maxwell AFB, Montgomery, Alabama, the Air War College is the foremost center for airpower education and thought. Maxwell AFB is also home to the other two major professional officers' schools, Squadron Officer School (SOS) and the Air Command and Staff College (AC&SC). I had attended SOS in residence as a young captain, 14 years before. The second, AC&SC, I had only completed by correspondence.

The Air War College curriculum is designed to enable the select student body to develop the knowledge, skills and attitudes appropriate for senior positions in the profession of arms. That objective was to be achieved through intensive academic challenges, complex practical exercises, and direct interactions with top government, military and industry leaders. Attendance at AWC, in short, was intended by the

Air Force to be a time of acquiring new personal skills and insights, and recharging one's batteries for more challenging, higher level future assignments.

We had found a comfortable rental house, had the kids in the local public schools, and spent the year following a busy but comfortable routine. Throughout the year, one of Ann's main activities outside the home was to support our daughter's Brownie troop. On one unforgettable weekend, I dropped them both off at a scout campground where the mothers and daughters were planning a two-night camping experience. When violent thunderstorms and mosquitos turned the weekend into a survival horror, I returned to find the camp in almost total disarray. The young girls, charged with adrenalin, had stayed up virtually all night, while the mothers were at the point of exhaustion. Looking back on it, we could see the humor in the situation, but at the time it was not amusing at all.

Chris and Annie made good grades in the public schools, although we felt that they had not been sufficiently challenged. Things had gone smoothly at school, except for one day when Annie came home from the sixth grade, crying. The question of aviation pioneers had come up in class, and she had proudly volunteered what she knew about Alberto Santos Dumont, the Brazilian "Father of Aviation." Santos Dumont was the first person ever to think of making a cigar-shaped balloon that you could steer and he also designed and flew his own heavier-than-air aircraft, so Brazilians call him the "Father of Aviation." Sadly, she had been rudely ridiculed for knowing nothing about the famous Wright Brothers.

Another memorable incident occurred when our next door neighbor, a student at AC&SC, invited us to join with a group of his fellow classmates, including some foreign students, for a late afternoon cookout. Before the guests arrived, my neighbor and I had spent a while in his back yard, chasing and wrestling with his Golden Labrador Retriever. After the dog had been banished to the garage, the guests began arriving. Later, after we had all eaten our fill and the party was winding down, all sixteen or so of us were relaxing in the rather small living room, telling stories and sharing experiences. My neighbor and I were crowded together on the couch, with a Pakistani officer tightly squeezed between us.

When it was his turn to share with the group, the Pakistani assumed a rather serious demeanor and said that he wanted to share with us some of the tenets of his Muslim faith. Much to my horror and that of the party host, he proceeded to describe in excruciating detail, the extreme abhorrence that he had of having any contact whatsoever with dogs, how such contact could cause him to become violently ill, and how clothes that had come in contact with dogs would have be burned. By summoning up heroic levels of self control, neither one of us betrayed what we were thinking and feeling.

A short while later, the evening nearly ended in a fiasco, when a Portuguese officer, speaking in a quiet, heavily-accented voice, offered to demonstrate a uniquely-Portuguese lament called a "fado." Everyone immediately cried, "Oh, yes . . . let's hear one!" He immediately proceeded to demonstrate, raising his voice to what can only be described as a very loud "anguished wailing." Moments later, another wailing could be heard, as our host's two young children protested at having been awakened so abruptly. The party broke up shortly thereafter.

My daily routine as an AWC student varied little. For several hours each morning, the entire student body of 288 officers from all services and a few civilians, attended lectures and participated in lively question and answer ("Q&A") sessions in the main auditorium. During the year, those lectures were presented by AWC faculty members, supplemented each week by one or two very senior outside guest speakers. The noontime was spent jogging outside the Base Gym, followed by a brown bag lunch. The afternoon hours, except for one day each week, were then spent working as a part of a 12-person seminar group, lead by a single Faculty Seminar Leader. One afternoon each week was usually free for physical fitness activities or personal business. Evening classes with Troy State University several nights each week, during which I earned a Master of Science degree, were also a part of my routine.

The entire AWC student body was divided into separate seminar groups comprised of individuals from many diverse backgrounds. The student body included male and female lieutenant colonels and full colonels from all branches and specialties of the US Armed Forces. Specifically, the Class of 1976 had 235 Air Force officers, 13 officers from the US Navy, 13 officers from the US Army, six from the US

Marine Corps, one from the US Coast Guard, nine US government civilians, and eleven foreign officers.

My own seminar group, Seminar #12, was lead by a former fighter pilot and included two other fighter pilots (one of whom had flown off aircraft carriers with the US Navy), two navigators, a non-flying US Marine Corps officer, and three other non-flying individuals (medical admin, a finance officer and a weather forecaster). The remaining seminar members were pilots who had served in various units with diverse flying missions. Despite our dissimilar backgrounds, or perhaps because of them, all members of the seminar group developed strong bonds of respect and friendship as we worked through the many challenges arranged for us by the faculty.

Our faculty seminar leader, Colonel James H. "Jim" Brocks, was a superb leader and consummate teacher. Each afternoon, we would convene in our seminar room and Jim would kick off the discussion, using the morning's lectures as a point of departure. Competition was keen between seminar groups of the Class of '76 for occasional awards and for overall academic achievement, and we freely attributed much of our group's success to Jim's leadership. Very early in 1976, we learned that after our class graduated in May, Jim would be leaving for a Security Assistance assignment in Africa, something for which he had long been hoping. As an African-American from Alabama, that assignment would be a personal high point in his Air Force career.

Our excitement for Jim came to a sudden, shocking end on 3 April 1976, when both he and one of his daughters were killed in a tragic aircraft accident. In preparation for his pending assignment, Jim had rented a twin-engine private plane that had an engine failure, causing the crash. We all felt his loss terribly, and attending his memorial service in the Base Chapel was a wrenching and emotional ordeal.

One member of our seminar group was a bit of a celebrity. He was Parvis Gohary, a colonel and highly experienced fighter pilot in the Imperial Iranian Air Force. For reasons unknown to us, he had very close ties with the Shah of Iran, and when General Davis C. Jones, the US Air Force Chief of Staff had visited Iran, Parvis had served as the official escort. Parvis had met his American wife, Mary, when he was going to language school at Lackland AFB, years before. Years later, I learned that Parvis, his wife and daughters were all able to narrowly escape from Iran and make their way to the US after the Shah was assassinated.

The US Marine in our seminar group was USMC Lieutenant Colonel Louis H. "Lou" Buehl III. Although soft spoken, Lou was the very image of a thoroughgoing military professional. He had multiple combat tours in Vietnam, had commanded legendary Marine divisions, was an avid student of military history and most endearingly, was a very warm and personable individual. While we all had no doubt that he would move up well in the Corps, history was to show that we had greatly underestimated his rise.

Only eleven years later, in 1987, he had risen to the rank of Lieutenant General and had become the Chief of Staff of the US Marine Corps, and was the third highest ranking officer in the USMC, behind only the Commandant and Assistant Commandant of the Corps. Tragically, only one year later, Lou unexpectedly died of a stroke at age 56 at Bethesda Naval Hospital, leaving his wife and four daughters. The world lost a wonderful person when Lou Buehl passed away.

Several times each week during the morning sessions in the big auditorium, prominent guest speakers made formal presentations on a "non-attribution" basis, invariably followed by an unrestricted question and answer period. Both were always interesting, and sometimes even inspiring. We heard from such speakers as the Army and Air Force Chiefs of Staff, the Navy CNO, the Commandant of the US Marine Corps, the Head of the National Security Agency (NSA) and many others. One of the first guest speakers to make a strong impression on the class was the Air Force Inspector General, Major General John P. Flynn. While his comments regarding the functions of the Inspector General Office were germane, it was the Q&A session that was most compelling. Here was an officer who had flown the P-51 in WWII, the F-80 in Korea, the F-105 in Vietnam, and had been a POW for five years in the Hanoi Hilton. His comments were by no means merely "war stories." Rather, his remarks were filled with practical and invaluable advice for anyone facing difficult challenges. I felt a special rapport with him because his signature was on the USAF "Well Done" Award that I had received eleven years earlier, after my U-2 emergency.

Another compelling guest speaker who generated considerable interest was the noted management expert, Cornell University's Doctor Kenneth H. Blanchard. His theories and conceptual model describing the dynamics of human motivation were revolutionary, and many of my classmates and I found them to be extremely persuasive. Indeed, his ideas were extremely helpful to me in the formation of my own personal belief system regarding leadership and management.

Another noteworthy event at AWC was the time General Alexander M. Haig, Jr. spoke to the class. At the time of his engagement with us, he had already been the White House Chief of Staff for two presidents, and was currently the Supreme Allied Commander, Europe (SACEUR). Because of his name recognition, his upcoming appearance gave rise to considerable discussion, most of it, I regret to say, was somewhat negative.

Everyone, it seemed, viewed him with some disdain, viewing him as a political hack, and certainly not a serious military professional. But at the end of more than two hours, his total command of absolutely every aspect of his current SACEUR assignment and his masterful and comprehensive responses to every question asked, left us all in awe. Nine years later, I was to meet then-Secretary of State Haig at a small cocktail party in the Manila Hotel in the Republic of the Philippines. He was still very impressive.

One of the guest speakers (who will remain nameless) reminded me of the saying, "What you are, thunders so loud, I cannot hear what you are saying." I refer to a former SAC DCS/Operations, a three star general with whom I had served when I was at SAC and whom I had seen in action on numerous occasions. A large, burly man, this general earned his nickname of "Growly Bear" because of his rough, ill-tempered manner. The right side of his desk in SAC headquarters had a large telephone console nearly 18 inches high. It was not unusual for him to turn to that console and make calls and carry on conversations in the midst of briefings being presented to him. On one occasion that I personally witnessed, that happened to a young major. When the major hesitated and then respectfully suspended his briefing until the general's conversation had ended, the general impatiently motioned for him to continue, all the while paying no attention at all to the briefing. A minute or so later, after it was obviously pointless for the major to continue the briefing, he hesitated again. At that, the general angrily shouted at the major: "Get out!" That remains a vivid and very distasteful memory. Displays of such discourtesy and contempt for subordinates by those with higher rank are, in my opinion, beneath contempt. Thankfully, I can honestly say that the vast majority of the senior officers with whom I came in contact during my career were exact opposites of the example that I have just given.

Ann's parents, Henry and Lucy Fairburn, were great admirers of Alabama's Governor George Wallace. So, during one of their visits with us in Montgomery, we all dressed in our Sunday best—and I in uniform—and had a private meeting with him and one of his aides in the Governor's Residence. Although confined to his wheel chair and extremely hard of hearing, the Governor could not have been more cordial. Greeting us with a strong, clear voice, he explained to our daughter, "I'm in this wheel chair cuz I got shot!" The visit was a huge success—especially for Ann's parents.

Several nights each week and on some weekends, I attended classes in the Troy State University post graduate program leading to a Master of Arts degree in Personnel Guidance & Counseling. While I admittedly wanted the advanced degree mainly to enhance my career prospects, the practical skills and background knowledge gained while earning that degree were immeasurably useful and applicable to situations that I later faced in all of my later Air Force assignments.

About a month before graduation, we were presented with an unusual and unanticipated academic requirement. Upon arrival in our seminar room one afternoon, we were greeted by our faculty seminar leader showing us a stack of blank "blue books" on the table and announcing that each of us had exactly two and one half hours to write a composition entitled "A Personal Management and Leadership Philosophy."

The requirement to spontaneously create such a framework and present it in a coherent manner under the stringent time constraints seemed like an unreasonably difficult task. After spending nearly an hour, furiously marshaling my thoughts and ideas related to management and leadership, and motivated by a morbid fear of failure, I began to write.

The result was a document with which I was quite pleased and which still accurately expresses the essence of my beliefs. The first paragraph of the document reads as follows:

> "1. *Introduction—the Philosophical Bedrock* My point of departure for this paper is my unqualified belief in the dignity and worth of the individual. I believe that Man was put on earth by a benevolent Creator, with the obligation of developing his own talents and abilities, and those of others, to bring about an ever-increasing level of individual fulfillment, opportunity and freedom. Our democratic form of government supports that proposition, and the traditional concept of a "Just War" justifies and condones Man's participation in the profession of arms as a means of preserving the common good. As a professional officer in my country's armed forces, therefore, my behavior should always be consistent with those fundamental beliefs. Furthermore, they are the bedrock upon which my basic leadership and management philosophy rests."

Later in the paper, I listed and discussed five requirements for successful command:

> "Personal Authenticity . . . Professional Competence . . . Willingness to Challenge People . . . Indomitable Spirit . . . and Commitment to the Mission."

One of the graduation prerequisites for each AWC student was completion and faculty approval of a major research study or thesis, on any topic chosen by the student. My study was published as AWC/AU Professional Study #6115, *An Appraisal of United States Brazil Relations*, March 1976, 103 pages. The following were the titles of major sections of the study: Introduction . . . Brazil—An Overview . . . . US-Brazil Relations in Historical Perspective . . . the "Brazilian Miracle" . . . . Strategic Issues . . . . Conclusions and Recommendations. One of the main conclusions of the study, that Brazil would inevitably move beyond its "developing nation" status within a decade or two, has conclusively been proven correct.

The one year for the Woodhull family in Montgomery, Alabama passed smoothly and without any major upsets. Some months prior to graduation, my name came out on the full colonel promotion list, although the actual "pin-on" would not take place until some time in the following year. Having became a "colonel selectee," I was contacted by the special "Colonels' Group" personnel office in Washington DC to begin planning my next assignment.

My AWC Faculty Seminar Leader had already advised me that I would be invited to volunteer to join the AWC faculty if the promotion to full colonel came through. But having already spent three years in Brazil out of the main stream of the Air Force, an additional three years in a non-flying teaching position at AWC did not appear to be a sensible career move. I was far more interested in seeking something more challenging. Ann would have liked for us to stay in Montgomery, but she expressed no strong objection when the decision was made to decline the AWC assignment.

Shortly thereafter, another one of those never-ending blessings came our way when orders came for me to report to the Strategic Air Command (SAC) once again, this time as the Assistant Director of Operations of the largest tanker unit in the USAF, the 305th Aerial Refueling Wing, Grissom AFB, Indiana. The icing on the cake was that the position entailed a return to full flying status, something that was becoming increasingly rare for full colonels.

When AWC graduation, at long last, occurred in May 1976, I was designated one of the class distinguished graduates. The announcement letter from the school commandant, Major General Stanley M. Umstead, Jr. read in part " . . . Selection for this honor among 288 exceptional officers and civilians is evidence of distinctive overall performance on your part. I am confident that this year-long effort has better prepared you for the increased responsibilities that you will face in future assignments . . ." I rejoiced in the accomplishment, but was eager to move on.

Chapter Thirteen

HEARTLAND OF AMERICA

(July 1976-August 1978)

Returning to the Strategic Air Command (SAC) tanker world meant a return to an environment of relentless pressure and constant higher headquarters scrutiny. As a SAC KC-135 crew commander at Westover AFB more than ten years before, assessments of my professional competence and vulnerability to reproach were influenced almost exclusively by my own personal performance and that of my crew. Now, as the Assistant Director of Operations (ADO) of the largest tanker wing in the USAF, I would be judged by a far broader range of criteria involving the behavior, job knowledge and mission performance of every one of the more than forty Combat Crews assigned to the 305th Aerial Refueling Wing, Grissom AFB, Indiana.

There were two main "Swords of Damoclese" constantly suspended over the wing. The first was the certainty of the no-notice arrival at any time, day or night, of a team of inspectors from the SAC Inspector General (IG) to conduct an Operational Readiness Inspection ("ORI"). During an ORI, the wing would be evaluated through the sudden imposition of a very intense and sustained tempo of flying operations, exercises, intrusive inspections of all records, and tests of various kinds administered to all wing personnel.

The second major challenge for the wing would be the annual visit by the SAC Combat Evaluation Group (CEG). That group, consisting of highly-qualified flight examiner crews, flew standardization check flights with a majority of the aircrews and administered aircraft knowledge and tactical doctrine tests to all crews. Once again, the results of the CEG visit would essentially determine the reputation of the wing.

A very welcome part of the new job was to regain and maintain my status as a KC-135 instructor pilot. Because the airplane had undergone extensive upgrades including completely modernized instruments and addition of a larger hydraulically-powered rudder in the years since I had flown it, I was sent to report to Castle AFB in California to undergo KC-135 transition training as though I had never seen the airplane before. As soon as I flew the airplane again and experienced the ease of using the new, modern instruments and noted the performance enhancements, I was overjoyed. On top of it all, I looked forward to several weeks of following the training syllabus in an airplane that I already had mastered in the past.

Alas, it was not to be! After only a handful of flights, the instructor put me up for a final check ride, and shortly thereafter, I was on my way back to Grissom, much earlier than expected.

Exercising a division of labor through his staff, the DO of any flying wing and his assistant are responsible for continuous, round-the-clock supervision of every aspect of the flying operations of the unit. That responsibility includes personal oversight of the scheduling, command and control of all flights, management of flight crew training and standardization, and constant monitoring of the performance and reliability of all assigned Combat Crew members.

As the ADO and still a lieutenant colonel for some months before pinning on the new rank of a full colonel, I was the alter ego of the DO, Colonel Ralph Kivette. Ralph was from Alabama, had majored in animal husbandry and was really a farmer at heart. He would, at the drop of a hat, launch into a detailed explanation of the relationship between the price of feed corn and the decision about when to take beef cattle to market. Years later when he was about to retire, he was asked where he was going to go. Ruefully remembering the severe winters that he had experienced in Indiana, he replied: "I am going to tie a snow shovel on the front of my car and drive south on US31. I'll drive until somebody asks me, 'Whut ya got on yer car there, fella?' . . . . that's where I am going to retire." And he did.

So my duties as ADO involved constant interactions with officer and enlisted aircrew members, whether as a crew member during mission planning and on actual refueling missions, visits in the Alert Facility, in classrooms, staff offices or at social events at the Officers' Club. Those contacts often focused on both the technical details of our profession and just as often, on personal concerns and interests.

Whenever I flew with our crews, I know they felt understandably apprehensive because of their exposure to my direct evaluation of their compliance with the rigorous standards of aircraft control and all applicable regulations and procedures. For that reason, I always strove to put them at ease before the flight, but offered frank critiques following the flight, if required. What they might not have realized was the pressure that I felt to model the standards of precise aircraft control and standardization in my own flying, for which they were constantly admonished to strive.

Of course, there were times when I had to wear the "black hat." Like the time late on one windy night, when one of our instructor pilots decided to make two more touch-and-go landings with a student after being directed by the Supervisor of Flying on duty to terminate his flight because of dangerous cross winds. I headed the resulting formal investigation that concluded that the instructor had flagrantly disregarded a lawful order and endangered an aircraft and crew without any justification. My final investigation report forcefully recommended that he be subjected to a Flying Evaluation Board (FEB), which very well might have ended his flying career. The DO concurred in my recommendation, but the Wing Commander—after letting him worry about the possibility of losing his wings for several weeks—let him off with a written reprimand. I still feel that a bad precedent was set, but felt vindicated by the general consensus among the crews that he really should have been forced to meet an FEB.

On the personal side, more than once I was privately asked to comment on the merits of a career in the Air Force by junior officers who seemed wracked with indecision and guilt for thinking about leaving the service. They were generally surprised when, rather than giving them a sales pitch for staying, I would tell them that they only had one life to live and that they should think seriously about whatever they and their families believed would be most fulfilling. My simple message was that service to one's country in the military was certainly not the road to financial success, but the satisfaction that it brings could justify a career decision. It certainly should be a family decision.

We liked our Indiana home right from the start. Unlike many military installations, Grissom AFB had no seedy strip of gas stations, used car lots and honky-tonk stores right outside the main gate. Grissom sat right in the middle of beautiful Indiana corn fields on the west side of US Highway 31, midway on the 145 mile stretch between Indianapolis and South Bend. With a population of slightly over 10,000, Grissom was a comfortable community unto itself, and enjoyed excellent relations with the surrounding towns.

The nearest town, Peru (pronounced "PEE-roo"), was a delightful medium-sized town, proud of its nickname, "Circus Capital of the World," because of its having served for years as the winter home for a number of professional circuses. When prominent citizens are honored by the city of Peru, they do not receive a key to the city. Rather, they receive a Mahout's elephant hook, and I was the proud recipient of one. The local "Hoosiers" are hard working, conservative folk who exhibit all of the positive virtues of the heartland of America. And I have to mention that the pot luck cakes, pies and casserole meals brought by the local farmers' wives to church or office events were always extraordinarily attractive and delicious.

It was during our time at Grissom that the unique and understandably dissimilar personalities of our two children became more apparent. Our youngest, Annie, was now eleven years old and had always shown a penchant for organization, making checklists prior to our many household moves, and always happily keeping her room neat and clean. One of her favorite activities at Grissom was serving as a "candy striper" at the Base Hospital. There, from time to time I would see her in her crisp pink and white uniform, with clip board in hand, giving instructions to people twice her age.

Her seventeen year old brother, Chris, was more of a free spirit, happy with life and not terribly concerned about the future. Unfortunately, from his point of view, it always seemed that outrageous fortune always followed him, ensuring that he would pay for his transgressions. On one occasion, we had prohibited him from associating with a certain unsavory classmate. Days later, a friend of my wife unknowingly revealed our son's disobedience by saying that she had recently seen "our delightful son" Chris in a nearby town. What took the joy out of that news was the fact that he had been in the company of that very same "off limits" classmate.

On another occasion, Chris had been on restriction not to leave the base for some previous misdeed. Ann and I had to be away for two days, planning to return late on the following Saturday. He had permission only to take his car to work in one of the base mess halls, and then return to our quarters on the base. When we returned home on schedule, we noticed that he and his car were missing. Within an hour of our return, we received a call from Chris. In a very subdued voice, he admitted that as he was leaving his girlfriend's house in Peru that morning, he had inadvertently broken the ignition key off in the ignition, and was unable to start the car. *Outrageous fortune had struck again!* Happily, despite those embarrassing youthful lapses, Chris eventually matured into a solid citizen with a lifelong passion for helping others through non-profit endeavors.

Being a mother of two, and having been the wife of a KC-135 crew member ten years before at Westover, Ann had instant rapport with many of the young wives of aircrew members at Grissom. That made for many pleasant friendships and, incidentally, provided me with invaluable insights into the attitudes and opinions of many of the aircrew families.

During my tenure as the ADO, our crews performed exceptionally well during a demanding Combat Evaluation Group (CEG) visit. And, even more importantly, the entire Wing received top ratings in all areas following a very demanding Operational Readiness Inspection (ORI) conducted by the SAC Inspector General team. Everyone from the Wing Commander on down was proud and happy with those accomplishments.

Some months prior to that ORI, we knew that time was moving on and we were becoming more vulnerable every day for that all important test of our mission capability. In hopes that it would put us all in the right frame of mind, I had written the following article for the base newspaper:

DEATH AND TAXES . . . AND INSPECTIONS

If the pundit who made the famous statement about the certainty of death and taxes had been a military man, he might also have added " . . . and inspections." Inspections, staff visits and various exercises are indeed a very common, but frequently misunderstood fact of military life. The inspector's purpose in life is not, as some believe, to harass and make life difficult for others. Believe it or not, the inspector's main concern and your main concern are ultimately the same: a high degree of mission effectiveness.

A commander in higher headquarters may know and appreciate that you are getting the job done on a day to day basis. But he has to know that your whole operation is solidly and efficiently run beneath the surface, too. Only then can he have unqualified confidence in your ability to accomplish the mission effectively regardless of the circumstances.

SAC aircrews have a saying: "Every flight a Standboard." This means that if they plan and fly every mission just as though a flight inspector were looking over their shoulder, then the regular annual flight check will be a breeze. Doing the job right the first time, ALL THE TIME, eliminates the need to remember anything special or do anything different when you are being observed by an inspector.

When a shop or work center is well run, the people well motivated, safety-conscious and proud of the work they turn out, the arrival of an inspector is no cause for concern. An inspection merely gives them the opportunity to demonstrate what they already know: That the commander up the line can have complete confidence in their ability to safely and efficiently "hack" the mission.

You and the inspector are teammates, both working to win the same ball game. The next time you talk to an inspector, don't hesitate to let him know that you appreciate that fact.

That ORI is seared into my memory for one reason having nothing to do with the actual inspection itself. The IG team had arrived without prior notice a few minutes after midnight to kick-off the two week inspection visit. Several hours later, with the unit on full alert, the entire Wing staff was in the Wing Command Post reviewing the intense preparations underway for the two weeks to follow. I was seated at a desk facing the large display panels on the stage of the Command Post. Suddenly, without any warning, I had the distinct impression of having been stabbed in my left side with an ice pick. The pain was as sudden as it was excruciating, causing me to look to my left in disbelief and slump over in a dizzy haze. I was experiencing my second kidney stone attack.

After being driven to the Base Hospital for some pain medications, I spent the next several hours in quarters, waiting for the repeated surges of pain to subside. The ORI went on without me for about one day, when I was able to return to duty, a little shaky, but otherwise fully able to function. Later, I was to learn that in my case, the painful symptoms occur only when the stone is departing the kidney. Two weeks later, I passed the stone with little or no discomfort.

One evening in July 1977, Ann and I were surprised to see Colonel Buzard, the Wing Commander, drive up to our home in Base Housing. Standing with me in the kitchen, he asked me if we wouldn't like to move to Cannon Row, the area in the housing area reserved for the most senior officers. Like a dunce, I told him that we were very comfortable in our current quarters, so he simply laughed and said that we would have to move anyway, because of my new job! That is how I learned of my promotion to be the Commander of the 305th Combat Support Group, or Base Commander, for short.

Being the Base Commander of Grissom AFB was like being the mayor of a small town. In that position, one became the one-man embodiment of authority on the base, with very broad responsibilities. My official duties ran the gamut from the obvious community relations role to supervision of every conceivable Wing support function, including Base Civil Engineering, courts marshal convening authority, government civilian personnel, law enforcement, housing, recreation facilities, the Base Exchange, commissary, etc. In shouldering those responsibilities, I was extremely fortunate to have inherited a world class team of officers and NCOs to manage those functions.

As the Base Commander, my flying status was suspended. But I hardly missed it, since the job was too all-encompassing. To stay on top of things and to let people at all levels know that their efforts were appreciated, I made it a practice to pay informal personal visits to workers at all hours and in many out-of-the-way places. Late night favorites of mine were visits to the base Main Gate, Commissary stockers working in the middle of the night, guest quarters receptionists, the all-night flight line sentries in the cold and dark guarding the Alert Force, the numerous maintenance shops, and the Security Police "guard mount" shift changes at 4:00 AM each morning. The motivation for that practice of visits can be understood by reading the following article that I wrote for the base newspaper:

Combat Support Group Commander's Corner

Attention all commanders and supervisors: I would like to put in a word for someone you may not have given much thought to lately, the guy or gal in your organization who quietly endures life's frustrations and simply does his or her job, day after day. I know that the pressures of your job force you to spend most of your time dealing with problem situations and problem people, but please don't forget the silent majority that gets you your good report card.

Motherhood? You bet, but ask yourself when the last time was that you took a few moments out of your busy schedule conversing with some of your folks with no other objective in mind other than to show an honest interest in them and express simple appreciation for the job they're doing?

And another thing. We are all so results-oriented these days that we've just about lost the ability to pass out a simple compliment without adding some reference to deficiencies or needed improvements in other areas. Some of the time, at least, let it all be good news. Our people here at Grissom are bright, loyal and hard-working. When I look at the unselfish and dedicated way that they do their jobs, and perform additional volunteer tasks as well, I am deeply grateful. Please help me to express that gratitude.

To welcome newcomers, I instituted a policy of holding an informal coffee and donuts meeting with all newly-assigned personnel to Grissom each week. Most were very young, first term enlistees, who needed to be disabused of any false impressions they might have had about tolerance for misbehavior, now that they were out of Basic Training and were in the "real Air Force." Like any community of Grissom's size, we certainly experienced occasional accidents and incidents, but generally, the order and discipline of life on the base remained well above desired standards.

Some of the tasks that came my way were rather unorthodox. More than once, I was asked by a worried parent to have a few words with a young person who needed some counseling. In other cases, more serious instances of abuse or dysfunctional relationships had to be confidentially investigated and referred to proper authorities. In order to legally certify the Security Police drug-sniffing dogs, it fell to me to periodically test the dogs and their handlers so that their discoveries would hold up in court. The procedure was for me, unobserved by anyone, to cleverly hide a packet of illicit drugs in a secluded section of a building, and then to observe the dog and handler attempt to find it. They always did.

The severe winter of 1979 created a memorable and difficult situation for the base. The prolonged and severely cold weather that year caused dangerously low coal supplies in the state, resulting in an Indiana State Utilities Commission edict for all industrial power consumers to reduce their total electrical power consumption by 20 per cent within one week. After much agonizing study, my Base Civil Engineer determined that the only possible way that we could achieve such a reduction without impacting our military mission was to close all of the non-appropriated fund activities on the base, including the NCO Club, Officers' Club, snack bar, Base Library and Base Gymnasium. Just about everyone on base depended on those facilities, especially during the winter months, so base morale would inevitably be impacted. Worse, since nearly all of the employees at those facilities were the wives of sergeants on the base, those closures were going to cause severe financial hardship for a large number of families.

Here was a really difficult, no-win situation. Finally, I decided to face the music by calling a meeting of all affected individuals, civilian and military to field questions, explain in person what was happening, and ask for their understanding and support. The meeting was held in the NCO Club filled to the rafters and while it had the potential of being a disaster, it resulted in a very positive acceptance of our situation and determination to see it through. After nearly six weeks, the crisis was resolved and things returned to normal. The Grissom community had pulled together admirably.

It was during my service as Base Commander that a very dark cloud passed over our family in the form of a breast cancer diagnosis for Ann. The fateful day came when we had to travel to Wright-Patterson AFB in Ohio for the surgery. I was informed that the cancer was confirmed during the first stage of the surgery, so as Ann had instructed beforehand, I acknowledged the fact and asked them to continue with whatever had to be done. We were very fortunate in that no radiation or chemotherapy was ever required. In typical fashion, Ann's spirits never flagged, she enthusiastically underwent reconstructive surgery over some months and she remains strong and vibrant to this day. Her full recovery has been just another of God's never ending blessings.

It was at Grissom that Ann discovered and enjoyed an unusual talent for acting. The state of Indiana has a strong tradition of excellent amateur theater, even boasting of a state-wide Community Arts Academy. And, as a matter of fact, on our very first evening at Grissom, we had attended an amateur production of the play, *1776*, the acting and staging of which were worthy of a Broadway company. In seeking an enjoyable diversion, Ann became interested in an amateur theater group in Peru and very quickly was cast and drew acclaim as the rather stern German housekeeper, Frau Schmidt, in a production of *Sound of Music*.

Later, in two other productions, she played the part of a philandering housewife in *How the Other Half Loves* and a nosy neighbor in *Never Too Late*. With regard to the Frau Schmidt part, for which she won the Indiana Community Arts Academy "Best Supporting Actress" award that year, I used to joke that she didn't need to act, she could just be herself. That, of course, was far from the truth. The wonderful thing about seeing Ann on stage was how she came out of herself and made the role she was playing come to life. Some years later, in the Philippines, she once again created a very different persona in a play. That time it was the flamboyant Southern Belle, Sally Cato, in a production of the play, *Auntie Mame*.

The months rolled on, and I began to receive indications from the Colonels' Group who managed full colonel assignments, of a possible new assignment to a more senior position in another SAC tanker Wing. That news boded well for my chances of winning a promotion beyond full colonel. But, at that point in my career, Ann and I had already spent over ten years of my career in SAC, and we were beginning to wonder what possible other exciting adventures might be in store for us. Our positive experience living in Brazil years ago made another overseas assignment a very appealing notion. So, when the Colonels' Group mentioned an assignment involving a completely new mission— collecting human intelligence—and that required learning a new foreign language and living overseas, I was immediately interested.

Chapter Fourteen

ATTACHE TRAINING

(August 1978-December 1980)

After I had expressed to the Colonels' Group an interest in a follow-on assignment other than SAC, they responded as expected, saying that staying in SAC was the most advisable career move. Willing to take the risk of leaving the "mainstream" for the sake of experiencing a new challenge, I asked for other alternatives. Noting my previous successful overseas service and high scores on the DOD Language Aptitude Test and at DLI-WC, they then advised me of an opportunity in the Defense Intelligence Agency (DIA). If able to satisfy the exacting interview and qualification requirements, they advised me I could be assigned as the Defense and Air Attaché (DATT/AIRA) in the Republic of the Philippines (RP).

In that position, I would be the ambassador's principle in-country military advisor. As the DATT, I would be in charge of four other officers, an Air Force major who would be my assistant, a US Army colonel Army Attaché and his lieutenant colonel assistant, and a US Navy captain, the US Naval Attaché. That Defense Attaché Office (DAO) was considered to be of critical importance because of the existence in the RP of two key US military installations in Asia, the two active insurgencies in the country, and because of the considerable influence of the Armed Forces of the Philippines (AFP) in the Marcos Administration.

The mission of any DAO is twofold. First, it serves to report routine background information on social, political and economic conditions in a country. But secondly and more importantly, its mission is to collect human intelligence by developing relationships with key host country civilian and military personalities. A common misconception about collection of sensitive human intelligence is that it is the exclusive purview of professional case officers—call them "spies"—who are able to pay hard cash to foreign sources they have recruited. In fact, by building friendships deep within the various alliances and cliques of the host country military establishment, military attachés are often uniquely positioned to obtain sensitive and highly-classified information.

That was certainly true in the Republic of the Philippines. At the minimal cost of minor personal favors and a meal here or there, attachés often win loyal supporters and friends who are more than eager to provide extremely valuable classified information of interest. I should mention the sad truth of the matter, however, that military attachés sometimes forget their raisons d'etre and become inappropriately devoted to the social activities and diplomatic events inherent in the job. But when they diligently apply themselves to writing and submitting intelligence reports keyed to validated DIA requirements, they render a critically important service to the nation. During my three years in the RP, I must have written the equivalent of the "Great American Novel" several times over.

Within several weeks, we took the first critical step in attempting to qualify for the attaché assignment. After submitting our own personal autobiographies as requested, Ann and I traveled on government orders to Headquarters, DIA in Washington DC to meet an evaluation board consisting of nine senior officers of all services. Headed by an Air Force major general, the board's purpose was obviously to observe our composure and demeanor under some pressure and to ensure that we understood the commitment of time and effort that would be required of us both by the assignment. Toward the end, when the questions turned to some light-hearted references to Ann's autobiography, I began to feel optimistic about our prospects for approval. Shortly after the one-hour board interview was over, we met the DIA Director, USAF Lieutenant

General Eugene F. Tighe, who confirmed the board results by asking us simply, "How soon can you travel?

The first order of business after finding a comfortable rental home in Washington DC was to begin a nine-month language course in the US State Department Foreign Service Institute. That was the first and indispensable step in what was to become a sixteen-month process of preparation for assuming the position of DATT in the RP. In 1937, the Philippine government formally declared Tagalog ("tuh-GAH-lawg"), one of the many regional languages of the country, to be the approved national language. Despite the fact that English is widely spoken in the Philippines, its use is very gradually declining, and many segments of Philippine society have little or no English capability. DIA policy, therefore, decreed that a comprehensive understanding and fluency in the Tagalog language, now called "Pilipino," were prerequisites to serve as the US Defense and Air Attaché (DATT).

The prospect of learning a new language had been one of the attractions of the assignment, and I was not disappointed. Tagalog is a Malayo-Polynesian language whose structure is based on "root words," with a syntax and grammar completely unlike English or any of the Romance languages of the western world. For nine months, my one instructor, Susana Felizardo, and I spent hours each day in progressively more complex conversations, much the way a child learns to communicate with family members. Initially, I had great difficulty in suppressing my other second language, Portuguese, but eventually things began to gel.

Tagalog has a uniquely appealing, almost lyrical way of expressing things. For example, in expressing frustration over inflation, a common expression was: "Tumataas ang lahat, pandak lang ang hindi"/ "Everything is going up . . . except for (the size of) dwarfs." Or, consider the rather prosaic expression for a lady of ill repute: "Kalapating mababa ang lipad" / "A low-flying dove." And we can never forget the two instances in which our English language has been forever enriched by Tagalog. When we use the expression "out in the boondocks," we are using the Tagalog word for mountain, "bundok." And when we say someone has lost his temper and is "running amok," we are using the Tagalog noun for an out-of-control madman, an "amok."

In the process of learning the language, I gained additional knowledge from my instructor that proved to be of great value on both the professional and personal level. That additional knowledge consisted of the profound differences between the unique cultural values of traditional Philippine society and our own. For that reason, virtuous behavior in Philippine society when viewed by a westerner, can often be seen as corrupt, self-serving and rife with unbridled nepotism. Specifically, with their genesis harking back to primitive antecedents long before the Spanish colonial period, there are two Philippine cultural imperatives that rank even higher than the preeminent western values of honesty, personal integrity and objective rewards for hard work. The top ranking virtue to a Filipino is to emulate and honor "pakikisama," or togetherness and solidarity in relation to one's own family or other significant group. That virtue can be better understood when one realizes that as far as I know, the very word and pejorative connotation of "nepotism" do not exist in the Philippine experience.

The second virtue, "utang na loob," honors *reciprocity* in personal relationships above all else. Failure to reciprocate a favor or to fulfill an obligation that one has by virtue of his status or relationship with another, is to be "walang hiya" or shameless, a terrible indictment.

Having passed the nine-month language course, the seven-month DIA specialized attaché course was a welcome change of pace. Twelve other attachés-to-be made up the class that received a wide variety of subjects ranging from diplomatic rules of engagement, the logistics of running a DAO, intelligence reporting procedures and the tradecraft of collecting intelligence. Some of my classmates were being sent to extremely hostile environments, so we learned about coping with those circumstances, as well.

With our attaché class, DIA tried something new and different. Because some past conflicts and misunderstandings had arisen between DIA attachés and CIA personnel in some overseas locations, a novel approach was to be applied to our class. To give us a better understanding of the CIA roles and methods, the members of my class underwent an abbreviated CIA case officer course at the "Farm" near Richmond, the facility where the Agency training takes place.

On one of the weekends during the course, the wives were invited to visit us and participate in a training exercise in the form of a cocktail party. Every participant, including the wives, was assigned a fictitious identity and role to play, and tasked with locating, identifying and eliciting specific information from other specific party attendees. Not surprisingly, even without any training, the women excelled in the area of shrewdly eliciting information from unwitting male associates.

The final training activity before leaving the US was to qualify in the Beechcraft KingAir twin-engine turboprop C-12. With its excellent performance and simplicity of operation, the C-12 assigned to our DAO provided invaluable access to the many small airfields located throughout the Philippines. We often flew the ambassador on his travels, which made us an integral part of his visit entourage. Whether flying to remote Batanes in the north or landing on a tree-lined grass runway in the south, the airplane was an indispensable tool and a pure joy to fly.

Chapter Fifteen

DIPLOMATIC ADVENTURES

(January 1981-Jan 1984)

After arriving in Manila, we quickly learned how those unique Philippine cultural values would manifest themselves. Even in our first weeks, we began receiving invitations to dinner from total strangers, but noticed that the evening would invariably end with a request for our assistance in obtaining a tourist visa to enter the US for a relative or very close friend. After the first few experiences, it became obvious that all of those invitations had not come as a result of our scintillating personalities, so we risked being "utang na loob" by tactfully declining most invitations from strangers. Of course, with time, understanding the culture became indispensable for accomplishing the objectives of my job.

Perhaps the most pleasurable aspect of living in the Philippines was the incredible musical talent that was universally in evidence. At every Philippine Air Force and foreign attaché social event, in private parties, and even in most restaurants, live music was always present, and I have never met a Filipino, male or female, who could not flawlessly sing on key. Because I had some experience and aptitude in that direction, and could do so in several languages, I was often invited to entertain and soon became known as the "Singing Colonel." On one memorable occasion, I sang a duet with Imelda Marcos in a late night party at Malacañang Palace. The song that we sang was her favorite, "Dahil Sayo"/Because of You.

At the start of our tour in the RP, Ambassador Richard Murphy was the Chief of Mission. He was succeeded after 18 months by Ambassador Michael Armacost. Both gentlemen were distinguished career diplomats with incredible personal and professional credentials, and both were exceptionally warm and approachable. The ambassador's visits with local communities throughout the country always included an interesting mixture of unsophisticated local hospitality and a studied formality befitting their high diplomatic rank.

One visit to a small town in Mindanao by Ambassador Richard Murphy stands out in my mind, never to be forgotten. The day was unbearably hot and muggy, with no cooling breeze. The ground outside was wet and full of puddles from an earlier rain shower. We were in a large thatch-roofed building with no siding and we visitors sitting on one side of a long head table, facing thirty or forty town officials seated in front of us, on folding chairs. We were separated from the city fathers by an area of roughly fifteen feet of empty concrete floor. After the interminable introductions were concluded, each of the more than a dozen local officials had a very long individual story to tell. The meeting went on and on, with everyone suffering terribly from the stifling heat and boredom from the lengthy speeches, but bravely attempting to maintain the appearance of rapt attention to each speaker.

Suddenly, a strange "splat" sound broke the silence. The reason was immediately apparent, since a very large, fat toad had just entered the room and landed on the concrete floor in front of the head table. Everyone's attention was immediately drawn to it, but no one overtly acknowledged its presence. As the speeches droned on, the toad slowly made its way across the room, and every time he took a leap, a nearly imperceptible "flinch" went through the crowd. The Filipino hosts, desperate to maintain the dignity of the occasion, stuck to the agenda with grim determination. But with every leap of the toad, the tension of suppressed emotions increased. Finally, the toad reached the opposite side of the room and exited the building by leaping into a puddle outside the room again. At that, the entire room erupted in an uproar of hysterical laughter. It was a priceless moment, and despite the uproar, the ambassador's dignity survived intact.

Management of household affairs in Manila could present unique challenges. Because of the heavy entertaining obligations inherent in the job, we were fortunate enough to have two live-in household helpers. Our staff consisted of Joanie, our cook, an older but wonderfully capable person, and Flor the housegirl, Joanie's teenage niece. One day, we returned home from a weekend trip to find Joanie nervous and very strangely silent. Ann's intuition instantly told her that something was very wrong.

As soon as Flor was out of the house, Ann approached Joanie for a quiet talk, woman-to-woman. In short order, it was revealed that in our absence over the weekend, my married permanent driver, Perry, had committed the unpardonable sin of kissing Flor in a moment of abandon. Terribly embarrassed by the disclosure, when confronted, Perry volunteered at once to request that the Embassy assign him to another household. But, after we learned that embassy personnel rules would result in his termination for his indiscretion, Joanie suggested an ingenious, if cruel, solution.

From then on, Perry was banned from entering the house and was required to take all of his meals in the garage . . . along with Gulo, the gangly female hound that we kept as a watch dog. Before long, we learned that Perry's punishment was the talk of all of the embassy drivers, and that "losing face" was a serious matter in the Philippines.

During our time in Manila, our daughter, Annie, was in her high school years in the American School. She rode the bus to and from the well-guarded school each day, with parents taking turns to ride along for extra security. Normal dating was out of the question because of security considerations, so group dating and at-home parties were the norm. Since summer jobs on the economy for the kids were prohibited, the parents' group raised money and arranged for $1.00/hour summer work experience positions for the kids in the Consulate and the Thomas Jefferson Library. All too soon, our daughter had graduated early from high school and was on her way alone to college in the United States. Our son, Chris, had not traveled with us to the Philippines, since he had already begun his college career before we left.

Two critically important political events that occurred in the Philippines can be said to have formed the bookends of our three year tour in the RP. The first event, in January 1981, the same month of our arrival in Manila, was the lifting of martial law that had been imposed by President Marcos back in August 1971. But the cancelation of martial law had little or no positive effect. Marcos' questionable overwhelming victory in a new national election six months later, in June 1981, only increased popular cynicism and frustration with the Marcos Government. Cronyism, corruption and immunity of the military to public accountability continued unabated. It was very disheartening to see that resentment toward the United States was also often expressed during protests against Marcos. One of the common slogans seen during the public demonstrations was "Lansagin ang Ditadura US-Marcos" / "Dismantle the US-Marcos Dictatorship." Those conditions and reactions to them, provided much of the material comprising my office's reporting for the next three years.

The second bookmark event was the dramatic assassination of former Senator Benigno Aquino Jr., moments after he had returned to the RP from exile on 21 August 1983. That event occurred less than four months before the end of our tour, and it became the catalyst for the ignominious downfall of the Marcos Regime, only 17 months later. After the assassination, Corazon Aquino, the senator's widow, immediately received the sympathy and political support of the people, and she subsequently succeeded Marcos as president of the country.

Ironically, only two weeks before the assassination took place, I had submitted an in-depth biographical sketch to DIA on the central actor in that tragic event, the Commander of the Philippine Air Force Aviation Security Command (PAF/AVSECOM), Lieutenant Colonel Luther Custodio. Like President Marcos and Chief of the Philippine Armed Forces General Fabian C. Ver, Lieutenant Colonel Custodio was a member of the Ilokano "in" group. Through years of faithful service, he had advanced rapidly and was a highly-trusted member of the elite clique of officers close to Marcos from Ilokos Norte. My report on Custodio had closed with a summary statement to the effect that if ever General Fabian C. Ver had a difficult, nasty task to perform, Custodio would be the ideal candidate to perform it.

When Senator Aquino landed at Manila International Airport on 21 August 1983, there was a fairly common hope that he would lead a popular and peaceful movement for political reform. Those hopes, of course, were dashed when he was shot in the head by an AVSECOM member as he was descending the sky bridge stairs toward the airport ramp. At the same moment, an unfortunate criminal in custody named Rolando Galman was pushed out of a panel truck at the bottom of the stairs and shot. The laughably improbable scenario thus presented to the public was that Aquino's assassin had been killed on the spot by the ever-alert AVSECOM security forces.

When I visited at the AVSECOM headquarters less than a week after the assassination, I was appalled to observe a self-satisfied, almost celebratory mood among the officers and enlisted personnel. Subsequent developments related to the assassination that ensued after we had returned to the US in January 1984 are worth mentioning.

In October 1984, a special commission surprisingly rejected the Government's implausible version of what had happened and formally attributed the assassination to a military conspiracy. Anti-Marcos protests and demonstrations continued and in December 1985, President Marcos convened a special three-judge military court that handed down an acquittal verdict for General Ver and twenty-five other military officers. That verdict, coupled with the bogus "snap election" victory of Marcos in February 1986, created such public outrage that they were major factors in the almost immediate overthrow of the Marcos Government. Finally, in September 1990 with Corazon Aquino now the president of the country, a special court finally convicted then-Brigadier General Luther Custodio and fifteen other individuals of the assassination of Senator Aquino.

There were two occasions during my tour in the Republic of the Philippines in which my assignment was very nearly terminated and I narrowly avoided being sent back to the US in disgrace. Both cases were resolved very much in my favor in the end, but not before some very anxious moments.

In the first case, it was the powerful confidant of President Marcos, General Fabian C. Ver, Chief of the Armed Forces of the Philippines, who nearly canceled my accreditation as a foreign attaché. Any attaché in a foreign country, whether military, commercial or cultural, is a guest of the host country and is bound by the rules of diplomatic reciprocity.

In my case, I was required to continuously inform the Philippine Attaché Liaison office of my whereabouts if and when I should leave the city of Manila. Late one Friday evening, however, informal reports came of small groups of terrified people straggling into the town of Baguio, 130 miles north of Manila. They reported lurid details of an atrocity in which a pregnant woman had been stomped to death by members of the Philippine Constabulary, the national police force. The few who heard of it were appalled and the Ambassador was privately heard to express concern and horror.

The information was being effectively suppressed by the Philippine officials, so the situation obviously required investigation. Under the circumstances, I had no choice but to travel north alone without informing the Philippine authorities of my departure from Manila. A couple of days later, I was back in Manila, having hiked up into the area outside Baguio with an American friend of mine and learned from some local male villagers, who were, in fact New Peoples' Army guerillas, that the assertions about the killing were essentially true. I was also able to learn something new, however, that had not yet leaked out.

It was the embarrassing fact that one week before the incident, a group of Philippine Constabulary soldiers had been surprised and suffered as many as seven fatal casualties in an ambush in the same area by a small band of New People's Army guerrillas. While that in no way justified the crime, it at least suggested that the incident had been payback against the locals for supporting the insurgents.

The day after I returned to Manila, I received a rather terse call from the Philippine Attaché Liaison Office, summoning me to a mandatory meeting in the headquarters of the Philippine Armed Forces. Somehow, the fact of my unauthorized trip north had been discovered. Upon arrival at the headquarters, I was advised that having flagrantly violated the travel regulations by going north to investigate the "outrageous assertions" on my own, General Fabian C. Ver was very likely going to revoke my credentials.

During our subsequent conversation, however, General Ver's ire completely evaporated after I was able to convince him that because of my investigation, the US Ambassador had come to understand and at least tacitly accept why the tragic events had occurred. It was, of course, a little white lie, but it got me off the hook. If anything, that episode had enhanced rather than weakened my personal standing with General Ver.

The second case of my near expulsion from the RP related to the Spratley Islands in the South China Sea, about 350 miles west of the Philippine island of Palawan. International diplomatic intrigue was involved because jurisdiction over the islands was claimed by no less than five other nations besides the RP, i.e., Vietnam, Malaysia, Brunei, Nationalist China and the PRC, each of which had occupied one or more of the islands.

The Republic of the Philippines referred to the area as Kalayaan or Freedomland, but claimed jurisdiction over only one of those islands, Pagasa. It was common knowledge that there was a small contingent of Philippine Marines stationed on Pagasa and that some sort of air strip had been built on the island. Beyond those meager facts, we knew very little.

For nearly a year, I had cultivated the friendship of the Philippine Navy admiral in Puerto Princesa, Palawan, who was the commander of the Western Command (WESCOM) having overall oversight responsibility for the entire Palawan area, including Pagasa. From time to time during our conversations, the subject of Pagasa support quite naturally came up, but I never expressed more than casual interest in its facilities and operations.

Then one day, as I deplaned from our C-12 on the ramp at Puerto Princesa for another scheduled visit with the admiral, I saw a young Philippine naval officer running toward me. Breathlessly, he motioned toward a twin-engine Philippine Navy *Islander* aircraft on the ramp a short distance away and told me the admiral was waiting for me. Finding the admiral at the controls, I had little recourse but to accept his invitation for a ride. After we became airborne and headed out over the water in a westerly direction, it became obvious that we were headed for Pagasa.

After an overwater flight of slightly more than two hours, Pagasa came into view and we landed. Enroute to the island, the admiral had mentioned that since we would be paying only a social visit, any photography or note taking would be inappropriate. For the next two hours, the admiral accompanied me as we walked nearly every square foot of the island, inspected the connecting trails, rudimentary pill box fortifications, buildings and airfield facilities, and interviewed the Philippine Marine detachment commander and other personnel. My mind was racing, trying to estimate distances and sizes of things being seen, and remembering facts presented. That evening, after returning to Puerto Princesa, I spent several hours making notes for the report to be written as soon as I returned to Manila.

The lengthy, very detailed report was finally written and submitted according to established procedures, with information copies going to various other agencies, including the US State Department and, of course, to the ambassador. The very next day, it was presented to me by a member of the ambassador's staff that in going to Pagasa I had exercised very poor judgment. As an official of the US Government, I was told, I had tacitly validated the Philippine claim of jurisdiction there, thereby potentially inviting diplomatic protests from all of the other nations with similar claims. In a subsequent rather painful conversation with the ambassador with whom I enjoyed an excellent almost collegial relationship, he expressed the view that my unauthorized trip to Pagasa might require that I be relieved of duty.

After two very uncomfortable days, another of those blessings upon which I have always depended, arrived. The positive resolution came in the form of a congratulatory wire to the ambassador from the US State Department, asking him to convey their appreciation to Colonel Woodhull for his recent excellent report containing information that had long been sought. Obviously, no one else was ever the wiser about my "social visit" to Pagasa, so nothing more happened.

It was in our final year in Manila that a serious health issue arose with Ann that required us to return twice to the US for delicate and dangerous surgeries. Very early in 1983, Ann began to experience increasingly frequent hemi-facial spasms on one side of her face. While they were thankfully not painful, their frequency and intensity increased to a point of being emotionally and physically intolerable. After unsuccessfully attempting to control the condition with medications, we learned of a revolutionary and extremely promising surgery for her condition available at the USAF Regional Medical Center in Biloxi, Mississippi. The delicate surgery involved microsurgery inside the skull on the brain stem and the placement of a miniscule piece of isolating material around a key nerve causing the problem.

With the decision to travel back to the US and undergo the surgery, we began what was to become a frightening and disheartening, but ultimately triumphant six-month adventure. After traveling together to Biloxi for the surgery, we met Dr. Clarence Watridge, the Air Force neurosurgeon who specialized in that new surgical procedure. The night before the surgery, he solemnly told us, "We need to understand that there are four possible outcomes from this surgery. First, there may be absolutely no positive result . . . . or we may achieve a temporary cure, but have the problem return in about four months . . . or Ann may suffer a total loss of hearing on one side, or . . . we may not have Ann with us tomorrow."

We were stunned to hear that brutally frank statement. But, he didn't stop there. He went on, "I will use all the skill that I have, but I wonder if you would mind if we pray." He then went on to offer a simple but moving prayer that dispelled our fear and filled us with a calm confidence that all would be well. It was a powerful and uplifting moment.

Everything did, indeed, go well and very soon we were back in Manila and hard at work again. After a few weeks, though, Ann was devastated to notice a gradual return of her previous symptoms. After going through the difficult surgery and recovery, and running the risks that we had run, it was a crushing disappointment. Just as Dr. Watridge had warily warned us, the problem had returned after only a temporary period of apparent success. But, Ann never hesitated. We went back a second time, had the very same surgery, and that time the full and permanent cure was achieved. The total permanent loss of hearing in one ear, however, did occur from the second operation. Under the circumstances, it seemed to be a fair trade. So, Dr. Clarence Watridge established a place in our lives as still another of those blessings which have so often come our way.

There was a mildly amusing preamble to that entire ordeal. Before we left the Philippines for Ann's first hemi-facial spasm surgery, she decided to see an acclaimed Filipino faith healer up in Baguio. It was a lark, but certainly couldn't hurt. After a short wait in the faith healer's waiting room, we were greeted by a young male attendant in what looked like a barber's white smock. After asking which of us was the patient, he started to escort Ann alone into the next room. I indicated that I would accompany her and he somewhat begrudgingly indicated assent. We then were introduced to the faith healer who, without any preliminaries, said to Ann, "Remove your shirt." She responded immediately that if that were to be a condition of the treatment, we would not need his services. With a frown, he motioned for her to lie on her stomach on the medical table in the middle of the room.

Ignoring me, the healer, speaking with his assistant in an authoritative way, began carrying on a discussion in Tagalog having nothing to do with the healing process then supposedly underway. Their conversation instead, was about a domestic feud that existed between the healer and his wife. As they talked, the healer slowly pressed his fingers on the back of Ann's neck, finally concentrating on one particular area. Suddenly, a small pool of blood appeared beneath his fingertips and the healer called to his assistant for a small basin. He then placed his fingers over the basin and announced that he had removed the "poison" from her neck. Since at the moment the blood appeared, Ann had said that she had felt something cold on her neck, the effect of a miraculous cure was seriously undermined in our eyes.

I am sure that what I had seen was the breaking of a capsule of some animal's blood. Nevertheless, with great ceremony, the remaining blood was cleaned up and the healer saw us back to waiting room while murmuring self-congratulatory comments about how well the operation had gone. I paid him the equivalent of five US dollars, feeling that the entertainment had been worth that much. In departing, I could not resist the temptation of addressing the healer in Tagalog, saying that it was a shame he was not getting along with his wife.

During the months following the Aquino assassination, large public demonstrations against the Marcos regime increased markedly. Rumors began circulating of political arrests and construction of a stockade in a jungle area northeast of Manila where dissidents were allegedly being held. So late one Sunday afternoon, Ann and I took a drive into the country in my unmarked staff car, roaming around in an abandoned area of bamboo groves on the chance that we might stumble on to something interesting. As I drove and Ann sat in the passenger seat with a camera in her lap, we drove around aimlessly for nearly an hour, seeing nothing out of the ordinary.

It was getting late and the light was beginning to fade when our curiosity was suddenly rewarded. Off to the right of the car, no more than thirty or forty yards through the trees, a fifteen foot high solid wall made of stout bamboo posts became visible. Our excitement suddenly changed to alarm, however, when I realized that a uniformed individual holding a rifle was sitting atop some sort of platform at the top of the wall. When I saw him turn his head in our direction, my heart sank.

Ann had the camera up, but when I saw that she was apparently in no hurry to take the picture, shifting back and forth with the camera from a "portrait" to a "landscape" orientation, I nearly had a heart attack. "Take the picture!" I cried, as I got the car moving. Afraid of causing the individual to panic by speeding away, I held my breath and slowly moved the car forward until he was out of sight. I filed a report, including one photograph showing the armed individual, but the follow-up on the report was left to others.

During that same time, through some civilian friends, I was able to have close contact with Corazon Aquino and some key members of the opposition to the Marcos regime. In fact, the last evening dinner party that we attended in Manila was hosted behind closed doors by Corazon Aquino and members of the outlawed Laban opposition group. Ann sat at her table, and I sat with Senator Aquino's elderly mother. Ironically, the very next morning, I was presented with the Philippine National Defense medal by Juan Ponce Enrile, then the National Defense Minister of the Marcos Government.

Every year, a formal Annual Intelligence Exchange was held with key Philippine military officials in Manila to discuss regional security matters. Organized by my office, the event was always chaired by Major General James C. Pfautz, the Chief of Intelligence of Pacific Command in Hawaii, who traveled to Manila each year for the event. It was through that association, as well as our day to day intelligence-related interactions throughout the year, that we developed a close personal and professional relationship.

As my tour in the Republic of the Philippines was drawing to a close, therefore, General Pfautz expressed an interest in having a hand in my follow-on assignment. Events unfolded, and before long, I was informed that orders were on the way for an assignment to the Air Force Technical Applications Center (AFTAC) at Patrick AFB, Florida.

When those orders arrived, they contained an unusual amendment. I was directed to report for a personal interview with the Chairman of the Joint Chiefs of Staff (CJCS), US Marine General John W. Vessey, Jr., enroute to my new duty station. During the conversation that took place in his Pentagon office, the general asked for my comments on the military situation in the RP, my candid assessment of several key Filipino military leaders, and an opinion regarding prospects for US retention of the military facilities there. It was an incredible honor and great professional pleasure for me to meet with General Vessey under those informal circumstances.

Chapter Sixteen

MONITORING THE WORLD

(JANUARY 1984-JULY 1985)

For many years, the Air Force Technical Applications Center (AFTAC) had operated and maintained a global network of nuclear event detection sensors known as the US Atomic Energy Detection System. Responsible for monitoring nuclear treaty compliance of other nations, AFTAC had worldwide sensors underground, in the oceans, in the atmosphere and in space. Included in the AFTAC mission was the monitoring of signatory countries' compliance with the 1963 Limited Test Ban Treaty, the Threshold Test Ban Treaty of 1974 and the Peaceful Nuclear Explosion Treaty of 1976.

When Major General James C. Pfautz had first mentioned AFTAC to me, he was still Director of Intelligence for Pacific Command in Hawaii. Little did I realize that within a month or two, he would move to Washington and be promoted to Deputy Chief of Staff for Intelligence of the entire United States Air Force (DCS/Intelligence).

The possible assignment to AFTAC had been immediately intriguing to me for two main reasons. First, because that organization reported directly to the National Command Authority in Washington, and had facilities and personnel scattered all over the globe. Second, I was intrigued because in his initial conversations with me regarding the assignment, General Pfautz hinted broadly that I would be a candidate to replace that organization's commander, who would be departing soon.

Obviously, the fact that Ann and I had positive memories of having met many years ago in Florida, also increased our excitement about the possibility of such an assignment.

A few weeks after General Pfautz first told me of the assignment, however, he ruefully informed me that the "nuclear gray beards" wanted an officer with a more extensive scientific and technical intelligence background. My service record was reportedly considered to be too "operations oriented." Nevertheless, I was more than happy to accept an alternative AFTAC position when General Pfautz told me in a personal note, " . . . were I a full Colonel, there would be no other job I would want . . ."

That alternative assignment was to be the AFTAC Director of Plans and Resources, XR, a uniquely influential position with a staff of twenty individuals with planning and oversight responsibility for an annual budget of over $130 million. Besides all of the obvious functions that the title implied, XR responsibilities also included public affairs, host country agreements for multiple foreign locations and special tasks for the Commander requiring objective coordination across the AFTAC staff. That last element of the job made the position virtually a special assistant to the commander.

The composition of AFTAC's manning, when compared with the average Air Force unit of the same size, was unusual. Of the 1400 total officers, enlisted and civilians of all ranks, thirty-five possessed doctorate degrees in nuclear physics, chemistry or other hard sciences. Nearly two hundred more had post graduate degrees in mathematics and science disciplines and the vast majority of the remainder were holders of four-year baccalaureate degrees. The heavy emphasis and reliance on science and technology gave the AFTAC headquarters the ambience of a major university.

As soon as I arrived, I could tell there was work to be done. The unit manning structure included several major directorates whose staffs had evolved into virtual fiefdoms. Even a casual observer could see that an inordinate amount of time and energy was being internally wasted competing for scarce resources. In short, while AFTAC was unquestionably effective in performing its very challenging worldwide mission, the organization had developed some structural deficiencies that were crying out for correction. Recognizing those troubling deficiencies, the DCS/Intelligence in Washington had recently directed that the AFTAC staff develop and implement corrective actions. That directive was issued just before I arrived, and its accomplishment would therefore fall squarely on my shoulders.

As had been expected, several months after I had reported in, AFTAC received its new commander, Colonel James R. Clapper. That is the same James Clapper who went on years later to achieve the 3-star rank of lieutenant general, having been, respectively, the Deputy Chief of Staff for Intelligence of the Air Force, Director of the Defense Intelligence Agency (DIA), and at this writing, National Director of Intelligence (NDI) under President Obama.

In tackling my new responsibilities and focusing on the review of structural problems, I could not have asked for a more supportive and understanding commander. Since both of us were relatively new to AFTAC, we were able to more objectively address the problems and win the acquiescence of established staff members to the changes that were developed. That early and successful implementation of the needed internal realignments was one of this assignment's most gratifying accomplishments.

Living in base quarters close to work and within sight of the Atlantic Ocean, Ann and I were happy to be in Florida once again. With our son, Chris, working in Washington DC and young Ann busy with school, Ann and I had virtually become "empty nesters." We found a wonderful church home at St. Mark's Episcopal Church on the mainland in Cocoa, made many new friends at work and in the local community and regularly had the thrill of watching the NASA Space Shuttle roar into the heavens. Shuttle launches were fairly common in those days and I could never understand why some individuals would hardly take the trouble to turn to watch it go. For me, every Space Shuttle launch was a stunning and inspiring thing to see.

In the succeeding months, the job kept me intensely busy updating AFTAC budgets and plans, hosting a worldwide commanders' conference, receiving senior US and foreign visitors and restoring some difficult negotiations that had become stalled between our organization and the US Space Command. Finally, a continuing day-to-day concern was the support and well-being of our many overseas sites with AFTAC personnel and equipment.

It was the XR responsibility for managing the many host country agreements allowing us to maintain our foreign sites that generated the trip of a lifetime for me. Depending on the size and type of detection equipment in use and the political orientation of the host country, AFTAC overseas detection sites enjoyed varying degrees of welcome. For some, the activity was virtually invisible to the local citizenry. For others, however, the presence of US military personnel and equipment caused unwanted attention. For that reason, it was imperative that we maintain positive personal relationships and work closely with senior host country officials to retain their continued support and protection.

After one or two potentially troublesome minor incidents had occurred at two overseas sites, and several important Host Country Agreements elsewhere were coming due for renewal, the decision was made that it was time for a senior AFTAC official to make direct personal contact with some of the foreign officials supporting us. It therefore fell to me to perform an around-the-world trip to visit a number of our sites.

Traveling west from Florida, I made a stop in Hawaii, and then proceeded to several locations in Asia, followed by India, then Europe, and finally, back home. The visit in India was particularly memorable, for a variety of reasons.

Arriving in New Delhi in a 747 Boeing jumbo jet at around five o'clock on a hot muggy morning, the entire plane load of passengers descended to the ramp down portable stairs and then lined up to be processed by a single Immigration Department official sitting at a single card table. The official was an extremely large Sikh in a wrinkled tan suit and hairnet on his huge beard. The wait was interminable, and the ludicrous situation approached the absurd as the people in line became aware that the lone immigration official was occasionally interrupted by men in dark suits with passports in hand, obviously obtaining expedited service for unidentified individuals still waiting in line. The rest of us waited our turn and eventually were free to go on our way.

After some morning meetings the next day, my escorts and I took some time off and drove south of New Delhi to the city of Agra, arriving early in the evening to see the incredibly beautiful Taj Mahal under a full moon. After spending the night nearby, we were up very early to see the Taj Mahal again just as the sun rose behind it, bathed in the mist of the nearby river. It was an incredibly enthralling sight.

After returning to New Delhi, I was taken in a rather melodramatic way to the headquarters of the Indian agency that was the equivalent of our CIA. After telling me that the physical location of their headquarters was secret, my hosts used a Volkswagen van with blackened windows to drive me around the city for nearly an hour and finally into a basement garage. After a short elevator ride, I was ushered into my senior host's office for a brief courtesy call. The following day, transportation was provided in a rather dilapidated Russian-made Indian Air Force helicopter to a classified location high in the southern slopes of the Himalayas. Those experiences and other similar incidents over the next couple of days gave the visit to India a distinctly "James Bond" feel.

The remainder of the trip was completed without incident, except for a few anxious moments on the flight from New Delhi to Frankfurt, Germany. During the daylight hours at the midpoint in that flight, one of the passengers excitedly called attention to the fact that we were being escorted by two fighter aircraft. They were easily visible because of the contrails streaming behind them, but they were never close enough to identify the aircraft type or country of origin.

As one might expect, an Air Force assignment in central Florida near the Kennedy Space Center was considered by many to be the ideal pre-retirement post. The large number of retired military personnel in the area around Patrick AFB attests to that fact. As much as we were enjoying the comfortable Florida climate and friends we had made, though, we began to feel restless for a change of scenery. Since my career had included no less than three major departures from the career mainstream, I had to candidly acknowledge that a promotion to flag rank was not likely. Barring that promotion, I would face mandatory retirement from the Air Force as a full colonel within the next two or three years. So, while still totally absorbed and committed to my AFTAC duties, the uncertainties of the future came more frequently to our minds, as time went on. One day, fate stepped in.

Throughout the ten or so years since living in Brazil, I had continuously exchanged letters with several of my former Brazilian

Air Force (FAB) colleagues. The motivation for doing so was mostly to exchange family news, but also to deter as much as possible, the inevitable deterioration in my Portuguese language capability, through disuse. In one of my late 1984 letters to a retired FAB colonel and close personal friend, I had mentioned that I would reach the 30-year milestone in my Air Force career the following summer. The response that came back several weeks later became the catalyst for a series of events that would culminate in my decision to retire from the Air Force after 30 years and seek new adventures in the civilian world.

That letter had come from a close personal friend, retired FAB colonel Joaquim Dário d'Oliveira, who after retirement had become the Director of Operations of the Galeão International Airport in Rio de Janeiro. Ann and I had met Dário and his family back in 1972 when he was the commander of a C-130 transport wing in Recife, Brazil. A year later, he joined the staff of the FAB Command and Staff College in Rio, and it was there that the two families built strong bonds of friendship.

Dário's letter had contained some startling news and a friendly suggestion. The news was that he had become aware of the fact that the FAB was planning to introduce aerial refueling into its operational capability. They planned to do so, according to Dário, by acquiring a small fleet of aerial refueling tanker aircraft from the Boeing Company. His logical conclusion was framed in the form of a suggestion. "You know our Air Force, you speak our language, you were an instructor pilot in the Boeing KC-135 tanker, and you are thinking about leaving the Air Force. Therefore, you should write to Boeing and offer your services."

Because of the uncertainties we felt about how I would end my Air Force career, his suggestion did get me to thinking. "Thirty years" sounded like a nice, round number. Writing a simple exploratory letter to Boeing to investigate Dário's assertion could do no harm, nor would it in any way adversely affect my standing with the Air Force. So, in the end, I wrote a simple letter to the Boeing Company as Dário had suggested. I did not even include a resume.

A month or so after dispatching the letter, I embarked on the planned three-week, around-the-world site certification trip previously mentioned. When I returned, I learned that I had been invited by the

Boeing Company to travel to them for an interview. Still later, I took some leave and went for the interview. The rest is history. Months later, on the first day of July in 1985, I completed exactly thirty years of active duty in the United States Air Force. At my retirement ceremony, Ann was presented with an official Air Force Retirement Certificate, as well. Signed by General Charles Gabriel, the Air Force Chief of Staff, that certificate called attention to her many years of hardship and dedicated service to our country. Needless to say, that honor was richly deserved.

Only a couple of days after that retirement ceremony and while still on terminal leave from the Air Force, I went to work for Boeing as a military aircraft salesman to foreign air forces. My first customer was the Brazilian Air Force.

Epilogue

As I stated at the outset, the purpose of this writing effort has simply been to provide a celebratory record of an eventful period of my life and that of my family, and to express appreciation to my loved ones, former associates and to a beneficent Creator for the challenges and joys with which we have continuously been blessed. Living and working with talented and dedicated Air Force colleagues of all ranks through the years was a rare and treasured experience. Recalling and recording some of the events of those years has been a rich, thoroughly enjoyable process and one that I recommend for its renewing and stimulating benefits.

Of course, chief among the blessings of recent years has been happily living with Ann and seeing our son and daughter develop in their own creative and unique ways. With six years difference in their ages, Chris and young Ann bravely dealt in different ways with the constant moves, extended separations and other unique challenges of military family living. But they have emerged from that experience as strong and contributing members of society.

I hasten to add that the years since our move into civilian life have continued to be filled with adventure, fascinating challenges and blessings. My second career, in aircraft sales with the Boeing Airplane Company, lasted nearly thirteen years and was similarly filled with interesting personalities, satisfying accomplishments and foreign adventures.

And the challenges keep coming, with continuing personal and professional associations related to the fascinating country of Brazil and its very attractive people. And every day as the years go by, the conviction grows that my sister was incredibly prescient over fifty-six years ago in believing that Ann Woodhull would be my ideal life's companion. She was, of course, absolutely right.